The Geneva List of Principles on the Protection of Water Infrastructure

International Water Law

Volumes published in this Brill Research Perspective are listed at *brill.com/rpwl*

The Geneva List of Principles on the Protection of Water Infrastructure

An Assessment and the Way Forward

By

Mara Tignino
Öykü Irmakkesen

BRILL

LEIDEN | BOSTON

This paperback book edition is simultaneously published as issue 5.2 of *International Water Law*, DOI: 10.1163/23529369-12340018.

Library of Congress Control Number: 2020941932

Typeface for the Latin, Greek, and Cyrillic scripts: "Brill". See and download: brill.com/brill-typeface.

ISBN 978-90-04-43828-6 (paperback)
ISBN 978-90-04-43829-3 (e-book)

This book is printed on acid-free paper and produced in a sustainable manner.

Contents

In memoriam of Professor Stéphane Doumbé-Billé (1953–2020) in recognition of his great research and teaching skills in international environmental law and international water law and his dedication in helping young researchers

The Geneva List of Principles on the Protection of Water Infrastructure

An Assessment and the Way Forward

Mara Tignino
Geneva Water Hub, University of Geneva, Geneva, Switzerland
Mara.Tignino@unige.ch

Öykü Irmakkesen
Geneva Academy of International Humanitarian Law and Human Rights, Geneva, Switzerland
oeykue.irmakkesen@unige.ch

Abstract

Attacks against water infrastructure and their weaponization have hit the headlines several times in recent armed conflicts. As opposed to the protection of water *per se* as a natural resource and as a vital human need which is dealt with rather extensively in doctrine, the protection of water infrastructure requires greater scrutiny. This monograph includes the Geneva List of Principles on the Protection of Water Infrastructure, drafted in 2019 under the auspices of the Geneva Water Hub, bringing together rules regulating the protection of water infrastructure under international humanitarian law, international human rights law, international environmental law and international water law. It aims at providing a holistic approach to the issue by clarifying international obligations and developing recommendations in the form of principles.

Keywords

water – infrastructure – armed conflict – post-conflict – international humanitarian law

 | DOI:10.1163/9789004438293_002

1 Introduction

1.1 *Challenges in the Protection of Water Infrastructure*

The targeting of water resources and infrastructure, as well as their utilization as a means of warfare, is not a recent phenomenon.[1] The earliest regulations of warfare include rules on the protection of water, especially on the prohibition of poisoning. This is affirmed by, for example, Alberico Gentili who refers to the prohibition of poisoning as a well-established rule of international law in 1588.[2] Today, more than 400 hundred years later, the protection of water infrastructure is even more relevant; recent examples of not only their frequent targeting, but also 'weaponization' demonstrate the importance of the question. For instance, the conflict in Syria, which has been going on for a decade in March 2020, has seen both weaponization and targeting of water infrastructure.[3]

1 Historically, the parties to the conflicts have made use of their own water infrastructure, especially in defensive acts. See Y. Sandoz, C. Swinarski & B. Zimmerman, *Commentary on the Additional Protocols of 8 June 1977 to the Geneva Conventions of 12 August 1949* (Geneva: International Committee of the Red Cross and Martinus Nijhoff Publishers, 1987) [ICRC Commentary], para 2142: '[I]t will be remembered that in the seventeenth century the Dutch, despite protests from the peasants, did not hesitate to flood part of their cultivated land by breaching the dykes in order to prevent the advance of adverse troops. In 1938 the Chinese authorities breached the dykes of the Yellow River near Chang-Chow to stop the Japanese troops, resulting in extensive losses and widespread damage. In 1944, again in the Netherlands, German troops flooded many thousands of hectares of agricultural land with sea water to prevent the advance of the enemy'. However, only a few studies are devoted specifically to the protection of water during armed conflicts. See, for example, M. Tignino, *L'eau et la guerre: éléments pour un régime juridique* (Brussels: Bruylant, 2011); T. Boutruche, '*Le statut de l'eau en droit international humanitaire*', 82:240, International Review of the Red Cross (2000) 887–916; A. Zemmali, '*La protection de l'eau en période de conflit armé*', 77:815, International Review of the Red Cross (1995) 601–615; W. Remans, '*Water und War*', 8:1, Humanitäres Völkerrecht (1995) 1–14; P. Stucki, *Water Wars or Water Peace? Rethinking the Nexus between Water Scarcity and Armed Conflict*, Programme for Strategic and International Security Studies, Occasional Paper No. 3 (Geneva: Graduate Institute of International and Development Studies, 2005); N. Jorgensen, '*The Protection of Freshwater in Armed Conflict*', 3:2, Journal of International Law and International Relations (2007) 57–96.

2 Alberico Gentili, *De jure belli* (1588–1589), Book III, Chapter IV, as referred to in Tignino, *L'eau et la guerre*, *supra* note 1, 128–130.

3 N. Damluji, '*Legal Analysis: Daesh Control of Watercourses in Syria and in Iraq*', 25, Pacific Rim Law and Policy Journal (2016) 331–363, at 333; United Nations Children's Fund (UNICEF), 'Eight Water Facilities Come Under Attack in Idlib, Northwest of Syria, Affecting Water Supply for Nearly 250,000 People', Statement (20 July 2019), https://www.unicef.org/mena/press-releases/eight-water-facilities-come-under-attack-idlib-northwest-syria-affecting-water, accessed 12 June 2020. See also International Committee of the Red Cross (ICRC), *Syria: Water Used as Weapon of War*, News release (2 September 2015), https://www.icrc.org/

Armed conflicts invariably adversely affect water infrastructure; they result in, for example, the destruction of and damage to water facilities and power plants providing the necessary energy to water supply networks and the collapse of water and wastewater treatment systems. They may also have negative impacts on the environment and the ecosystem of water resources, among others, due to the targeting of industrial facilities such as chemical and oil plants.[4] These, in turn, have severe consequences on the civilian population.[5] These consequences are more poignant in urban contexts due to the complexity of water infrastructure, its interconnectedness with other infrastructure and the high density of the population depending on it.[6] However, rural contexts bear their own specific difficulties, including due to reliance on water infrastructure for agriculture, sometimes the sole means of subsistence of the civilian population.[7]

The disruption of water and sanitation services affects all the population but some segments, like women, or vulnerable groups such as children, are disproportionately affected by these negative impacts. In rural places, destruction of or damage to water infrastructure may force women to fetch water from scarce and distant points, which exposes them to a higher risk of being subjected to sexual and other violence.[8] In both urban and rural contexts, a lack of access

---

en/document/syria-water-used-weapon-war, accessed 12 June 2020: 'The water supply in Aleppo depends on the operation of pumping and electricity stations but each is controlled by different warring parties. The operation of the stations is often used in a way to put pressure on the other side'.

4 This was the case, for example, in the conflict in Kosovo in 1999, when the attacks against industrial facilities situated along the Danube River caused the release of polluting substances in the river. The bombing of the Pančevo and Novi Savi oil refineries had further spread the fear of widespread ecological damage to water resources. See United Nations (UN) Environment Programme (UNEP) and UN Centre for Human Settlements (Habitat), *The Kosovo Conflict: Consequences for the Environment and Human Settlements* (Nairobi: UNEP and UNCHS, 1999), at 59–62.

5 See, for example, UNEP, *Environmental Assessment of the Gaza Strip following the Escalation of Hostilities in December 2008–January 2009* (Nairobi: UNEP, 2009), at 78. While here the focus is on the effects of conduct of hostilities on access to water, the latter can also be hindered in times of occupation, in violation of international humanitarian law and international human rights law. See, for example, Amnesty International, *Troubled Waters: Palestinians Denied Fair Access to Water: Israel-Occupied Palestinian Territories* (London: Amnesty International, 2009).

6 See in general ICRC, *Urban Services during Protracted Armed Conflicts: A Call for a Better Approach to Assisting Affected People* (Geneva: ICRC, 2015).

7 See, for example, Amnesty International, *Dead Land: Islamic State's Deliberate Destruction of Iraq's Farmland* (London: Amnesty International, 2018).

8 See, for example, United Nations, *Conflict-related sexual violence: Report of the Secretary-General*, UN Doc S/2019/280 (29 March 2019), at 16, 45.

to safe water for drinking and sanitation purposes may lead to the outbreak of water-borne diseases and exacerbate the spread of epidemics, which are particularly dangerous for children, as was witnessed during the cholera crisis in Yemen.[9] The complication posed by the disruption of water services for the provision of health services is thus twofold: a rapid increase in the number of patients and the lack of access to water by the hospitals themselves.

Some other challenges not specific to, but important for, ensuring the protection of water infrastructure are the protracted nature of the recent armed conflicts, in that they often stretch over several years, and the proliferation of actors involved, including non-state armed groups. These two factors mainly play an obstructive role in the maintenance of water infrastructure, which are in many conflict-affected areas in poor condition.[10] The dangers posed by the prolonged hostilities and the necessity to engage in dialogue with several and everchanging actors make it more difficult to reconstruct, repair and rehabilitate damaged infrastructure and continue to operate those which are functioning.

1.2 *Background of the Geneva List of Principles on the Protection of Water Infrastructure*

The initiative to develop a list of principles to address the need to strengthen the protection of water infrastructure emerged during the Think Tank Roundtable on the 'Protection of Water During and After Armed Conflicts', held in Geneva in June 2016 and convened by the Geneva Water Hub (GWH), which served to feed into the work of the Global High-Level Panel on Water and Peace.[11] In the context of an increased targeting and weaponization of water infrastructure, the GWH and its Platform for International Water Law, together with several

9 See, UNICEF, *Water Under Fire: Emergencies, Development and Peace in Fragile and Conflict-affected Contexts*, Volume 1 (UNICEF, 2019), at 21.

10 For example, the Independent International Commission of Inquiry on the Syrian Arab Republic, in 2016, reported: 'Continued hostilities have undermined efforts to repair, maintain and upgrade electricity production and water pumping and treatment facilities. This is particularly the case where water and electrical networks for a locality have fallen under the control of an opposing party'. UN Human Rights Council, *Report of the Independent International Commission of Inquiry on Syrian Arab Republic*, UN Doc A/HRC/31/68 (11 February 2016), para 82. See also UNEP and UN Country Team in Afghanistan, *Natural Resource Management, and Peacebuilding in Afghanistan* (Nairobi: UNEP, 2013), at 5.

11 Geneva Water Hub (GWH), *Protection of Water During and After Armed Conflicts* (Geneva: GWH, 2016) [GWH Report].

partners, took the initiative to develop the Geneva List of Principles on the Protection of Water Infrastructure.[12]

The Global High-Level Panel on Water and Peace was launched in November 2015 in Geneva and was co-convened by 15 countries at the initiative of Switzerland.[13] The panellists were appointed by the governments, but they served in their personal capacity. The Panel's work contributed to the efforts of other parallel initiatives built on the heightened focus on water in the last few years. In September 2007, the High-Level Expert Panel on Water and Disaster was established at the request of the UN Secretary-General's Advisory Board on Water and Sanitation. It is continuing its work to date. The UN and the World Bank convened the High-Level Panel on Water in April 2016, which concluded its mandate and released its outcome document on 14 March 2018.[14]

The main task of the Global High-Level Panel on Water and Peace was to study the water and peace nexus and to prepare a report including 'recommendations for water as an instrument of peace' within two years.[15] The Panel carried out its task by consulting with relevant stakeholders, including experts, policy-makers and civil society organizations. After meeting four times during its mandate,[16] its final report, *A Matter of Survival*, was presented in September 2017. The report's second chapter, entitled 'Into the Abyss: Water in Armed Conflicts', contained several recommendations, mainly addressed to the UN Security Council, including strengthening the respect for and implementation of international humanitarian law. The chapter also called on different actors to study the development of technologies such as the use of remote sensing and monitoring devices for the protection of water infrastructure and highlighted the need to support non-governmental organizations engaging with non-state actors, in order to ensure their respect for the law

12 For more information on the GWH and the Platform for International Water Law, see, respectively https://www.genevawaterhub.org and https://www.unige.ch/droit/eau/en/.

13 Cambodia, Colombia, Costa Rica, Estonia, France, Ghana, Hungary, Jordan, Kazakhstan, Morocco, Oman, Senegal, Slovenia, Spain and Switzerland.

14 See the High-Level Panel on Water, *Making Every Drop Count: An Agenda for Water Action* (*Outcome Document*) (United Nations Department of Economic and Social Affairs/World Bank, 2018).

15 Danilo Türk, 'Chairman's Foreword' in Global High-Level Panel on Water and Peace, *A Matter of Survival* (*Report*) (Geneva: GWH, 2017), at 3 [GHLPWP Report].

16 The Panel met in Geneva, Switzerland in November 2015; in Dakar, Senegal in April 2016; in San Jose, Costa Rica in December 2016; and in Amman, Jordan in May 2017. After the meeting in Dakar, the International Organisation of La Francophonie (*Organisation Internationale de la Francophonie*) referred to the work of the High-Level Panel in its resolution '*Eau, Paix, Sécurité*' adopted at the 16th Conference of Heads of State and government of countries with the French language in common, held on 26 and 27 November 2016.

and, ultimately, the protection of water.[17] In the follow-up to the report, the Geneva List project was launched by the GWH, which acted as the secretariat of the Panel.

Currently, several organizations are focusing on water and armed conflicts, either directly or indirectly. In direct complementarity with the Geneva List, the United Nations Children's Fund (UNICEF) launched the campaign 'Water under fire' with an advocacy alert during an event co-organized by the GWH, UNICEF, the Permanent Mission of the Kingdom of the Netherlands to the UN and the International Peace Institute on 22 March 2019. Within the context of this campaign, UNICEF published the first volume of a three-report series which focused on 'the humanitarian–development–peace nexus' in August the same year.[18] The second and third volumes of the series will be dedicated to the quality and capacity of the water, sanitation and hygiene (WASH) humanitarian sector and attacks against WASH infrastructure and personnel respectively.[19] On a more general level regarding the protection of water as a component of the environment, the International Law Commission (ILC) has been working on the protection of the environment in relation to armed conflicts since 2013. In June 2019, the Drafting Committee provisionally adopted the text and titles of the draft principles on first reading.[20] Likewise, the International Committee of the Red Cross (ICRC) is soon set to finish updating its Guidelines for Military Manuals and Instructions on the Protection of Environment in Times of Armed Conflict, dated 1994.[21]

The topicality of water and armed conflicts was also reflected in the agenda of the UN Security Council. The Council has expressed grave alarm at the attacks against civilian infrastructure, including deliberate interruptions of water supply,[22] and called on all parties to armed conflicts to comply with

---

17 GHLPWP Report, *supra* note 15, 31. Generally for the follow up activities and work towards the implementation of the Panel's recommendations, see Geneva Water Hub, *Determined Steps* (Geneva: GWH, 2019).

18 UNICEF, Water Under Fire, *supra* note 9, at v.

19 Information on file with the authors.

20 International Law Commission (ILC), *Protection of the Environment in Relation to Armed Conflict*, Doc A/CN.4/L.937 (6 June 2019).

21 ICRC, *Natural Environment: Neglected Victim of Armed Conflict* (5 June 2019), https://www.icrc.org/en/document/natural-environment-neglected-victim-armed-conflict, accessed 12 June 2020.

22 United Nations Security Council, '*Middle East*', 14 July 2014, UNSC Resolution 2165, UN Doc. S/RES/2165, Preamble. See also United Nations Security Council, '*Middle East*', 21 October 2011, UNSC Resolution 2014, UN Doc. S/RES/2014, para 8, urging 'all parties not to target vital infrastructure'; United Nations Security Council, '*The situation in Libya*',

their obligations under international humanitarian law.[23] In October 2018, the Council held an 'Arria-formula' meeting on water, peace and security, which focused on the relationship between conflicts and water stress.[24]

Beyond the actors traditionally working in the field of international peace and security, some international organizations have started working on the linkages between water and peace, including the UN Economic Commission for Europe (UNECE) and the UN High-Commissioner for Human Rights. In their meeting held in October 2018 in Astana, the parties to the UNECE Convention on the Protection and Use of Transboundary Watercourses and International Lakes noted the need to create bridges between transboundary water cooperation, conflict prevention and post-conflict reconstruction.[25] The UN Special Rapporteur on the Human Rights to Safe Drinking Water and Sanitation, on the other hand, presented in 2018 a report on the human rights to water and sanitation of forcibly displaced persons, which also included recommendations regarding situations of armed conflict.[26] In particular, he underlined the need to '[r]espect the provisions of international humanitarian law in situations of armed conflict, including by granting safe, rapid and unimpeded humanitarian access to those in need' and to '[a]pply the framework of the human rights to water and sanitation at all times—before, during and after emergency situations, armed or non-armed conflicts or disasters'.[27] This increasing interest by different actors on the linkages between water, peace and security is also of relevance for the realization of Sustainable Development Goal 16 on promoting peaceful and inclusive societies for sustainable development,[28] which

---

12 September 2019, UNSC Resolution 2486, UN Doc. S/RES/2486, Preamble, expressing grave concern over 'the targeting of civilian infrastructure'; United Nations Security Council, '*Threats to international peace and security*', 20 September 2019, UNSC Resolution 2490, UN Doc. S/RES/2490, Preamble, condemning attacks on critical infrastructure.

23 United Nations Security Council, '*Protection of civilians in armed conflict*', 24 May 2018, UNSC Resolution 2417, UN Doc. S/RES/2417, Preamble, paras 1, 4.

24 See Planetary Security Initiative, *Arria-Formula Meeting on Water: Peace and Security by the UNSC* (16 November 2018), https://www.planetarysecurityinitiative.org/news/arria-formula-meeting-water-peace-and-security-unsc, accessed 12 June 2020.

25 For the draft unedited decisions adopted by the meeting of the parties at its eighth session see, https://www.unece.org/fileadmin/DAM/env/documents/2018/WAT/10Oct_10-12_8thMOP/Other_documents_for_the_web/List_of_decisions_MOP8_12Oct_for_distribution_ENG.PDF, accessed 12 June 2020.

26 UN Human Rights Council, *Report of the Special Rapporteur on the Human Rights to Safe Drinking Water and Sanitation*, UN Doc A/HRC/39/55 (3 August 2018).

27 *Id.*, paras 68 (d), 69 (a).

28 United Nations, *Sustainable Development Goal 16*, https://sustainabledevelopment.un.org/sdg16, accessed 12 June 2020.

is directly related to ensuring universal and equitable access to water and sanitation for all.

1.3 *Methodology of the Geneva List of Principles on the Protection of Water Infrastructure*

The drafting process of the Geneva List has been led by the GWH and included collaboration with other academic institutions such as the American University of Beirut, the University of Amsterdam, Duke University, the University of North Hampshire, Leiden University, Lund University, the University of Léon and the University of Trento and international and non-governmental organizations, including Amnesty International, the Conflict and. Environment Observatory, the Environmental Law Institute, UNICEF and the United Nations Environment Programme (UNEP).

At the 2018 Geneva Peace Week, the GWH, in collaboration with UNEP and Duke University, presented concrete examples demonstrating the targeting of water infrastructure during armed conflicts in different regions of the world, including in South America, the Middle East, Northern Africa, and Europe.[29] Following the Geneva Peace Week, the Environmental Peacebuilding Association and the GWH joined forces to launch an Interest Group on Water to bring water to the forefront of discussion on peacebuilding strategies and conflict resolution mechanisms.

A 'zero draft' of the Geneva List was presented to a group of experts in December 2018. This draft was discussed during a two-day expert meeting bringing together academics and practitioners in Geneva. The detailed oral and written comments received during the meeting were very valuable and were implemented in a revised first version of the texts of the principles.[30] This first draft was also circulated among the experts for a second round of comments.

During the process of finalization, the authors also participated in several events, presenting the issues at hand and exchanging with various actors. A few of those events should be noted here. In March 2019, the authors held a webinar at the Environmental Law Institute in Washington, D.C. and participated

29 See, on the targeting of water infrastructure in the Middle East, J. L. Sowers, E. Weinthal & N. Zawahri, '*Targeting Environmental Infrastructures, International Law, and Civilians in the New Middle Eastern Wars*', 48:5, Security Dialogue (2017) 410–430.

30 The GWH's Platform for International Water Law wishes to express its deepest gratitude for the inputs received in the process of revision of the 'zero draft' of the Geneva List. A list of experts who participated in this meeting is available at https://www.genevawaterhub.org/news/round-table-geneva-list-principles-protection-water-infrastructures-during-and-after-armed.

to a World Bank Brown Bag Lunch dedicated to a discussion on the Geneva List. On 22 March 2019, at the above-mentioned co-organized event at the International Peace Institute in New York, the first draft of the principles was shared with the public. Finally, on 26 August 2019, the Geneva List of Principles on the Protection of Infrastructure, and its commentary, was launched during World Water Week in Stockholm. This document was also presented during the 33rd International Conference of the Red Cross and Red Crescent held in Geneva in December 2019.

1.4 *Preliminary Remarks on the Scope and Content of the Geneva List of Principles on the Protection of Water Infrastructure*

The Geneva List of Principles on the Protection of Water Infrastructure is a reference document prepared for the use of parties to armed conflicts, states, international organizations, policy-makers and practitioners working in the contexts of armed conflicts, including in pre- and post-conflict situations. It is the first text that systematizes the main rules applicable to the protection of water infrastructure during armed conflicts, especially in the conduct of hostilities, as well as in post-conflict situations, and sets forth recommendations that go beyond existing law.

The objective of the Geneva List is to gather in a single document the rules on the protection of water infrastructure under different branches of international law, namely international humanitarian law, international human rights law, international environmental law and international water law. The aim is not only to restate obligations stemming from different sets of rules and principles of international law, but also to demonstrate their interaction with and significance for one another. The law applicable to the protection of water infrastructure is thus presented in a holistic manner.[31]

The principles both reflect existing binding obligations and set forth recommendations. The rules stemming from both customary and treaty law are included either in the texts of or the commentaries to the principles and are formulated as obligations, using 'must'. The recommendations are developed in two ways: some are advancements to existing obligations and others are proposals which do not build upon existing obligations. These recommendations are, as far as possible, supported by practice from past and current conflicts and by references to soft law documents such as those of the International Law

31 A first attempt to systematize the law applicable to the protection of water during and after armed conflicts was presented in M. Tignino, *Water During and After Armed Conflicts: What Protection in International Law?*, 1:4, Brill Research Perspectives in International Water Law (2016).

Association (ILA).[32] In an era marked by the reluctance of states to develop international law through the traditional means of concluding treaties, one cannot emphasize enough the importance of practice and soft law. The desired improvement in the protection of water infrastructure can also be achieved by drawing attention not only to the international regulatory framework, but also to examples of practices going beyond the law. In the same vein, as reflected in the Geneva List, it is equally important to highlight instances of compliance with law and not only violations of the law; compliance begets compliance.[33]

It is often the case that damage to or destruction of water infrastructure also has negative impacts on the environment, first and foremost on water resources. Nevertheless, the scope of the Geneva List is limited to the protection of water infrastructure and installations essential to their functioning. The protection of water resources is dealt with, when necessary, in connection with the protection of infrastructure. This is the case, for example, in dealing with the proportionality of an attack which is expected to cause leakage of wastewater risking the contamination of a nearby water source. Admittedly, the Geneva List includes one principle entitled 'Protection of the environment'; this principle, however, deals with the *indirect* protection of water infrastructure by means of rules limiting the means and methods of warfare for the protection of the environment.[34]

The Geneva List focuses on the protection of water infrastructure during and after armed conflicts. However, due to their nature, some principles are also applicable prior to the onset of an armed conflict. For example, states are encouraged to establish joint commissions or mechanisms with a view to ensuring the protection of water infrastructure located on transboundary

32 For example, International Law Association (ILA), '*Resolution on the Protection of Water Resources and Water Installations in Times of Armed Conflict*', Report of the Fifty-seventh Conference, Madrid, 30 August–4 September 1976 (London, 1978) 237–239 [Madrid Rules]; ILA, '*The Berlin Rules on Water Resources*', Report of the Seventy-first Conference, Berlin, 16–21 August 2004 (London, 2004) 337–411 [Berlin Rules].

33 The 'IHL in action: Respect for the law on the battlefield' database which documents instances of compliance with international humanitarian law is a valuable project in this sense. See, for example, IHL in action, *Iraq, Computer Modelling in Collateral Damage Estimates and Choice of Weapons*, ICRC, n.d.), https://ihl-in-action.icrc.org/case-study/iraq-computer-modelling-collateral-damage-estimates-and-choice-weapons (accessed 12 June 2020): 'U.S. strategy avoided power plants, public water facilities, refineries, bridges, and other civilian structures'.

34 For an overview of the protection of the environment under international humanitarian law, see C. Droege & M.-L. Tougas, '*The Protection of the Natural Environment in Armed Conflict: Existing Rules and Need for Further Legal Protection*', 82, Nordic Journal of International Law (2013) 21–52.

water resources during peacetime. However, this temporal scope of application of the rules and recommendations are not reflected in the Geneva List in a systematic manner. This is a deliberate choice based on two grounds. First, factually, there is often fluidity between armed conflicts and peacetime; it may be difficult to pinpoint the moment where one ends and the other starts, and many situations are marked by cycles of conflicts. Second, legally, the obligations stemming from the rules governing the protection of water infrastructure do not always entail a strict differentiation between different phases. For certain rules, this is because they are applicable at all times, and even under international humanitarian law, there are rules that are already applicable in peacetime and continue into armed conflict. These include instruction of international humanitarian law to armed forces and dissemination thereof to the civilian population in general,[35] and the marking of works and installations containing dangerous forces, such as dams and dykes with the special sign.[36]

The Geneva List is addressed both to states and non-state actors, in particular non-state armed groups. This is particularly important considering that the vast majority of the current armed conflicts are of a non-international character. The fact that non-state armed groups that are parties to armed conflicts are bound by international humanitarian law is undisputed.[37] The roles of various non-state actors under other branches of international law differ, and for example the capacity of such actors, in particular non-state armed groups, to

35 Geneva Convention for the Amelioration of the Condition of the Wounded and Sick in Armed Forces in the Field (12 August 1949), Art. 47 [Geneva Convention I]; Geneva Convention for the Amelioration of the Condition of Wounded, Sick and Shipwrecked Members of Armed Forces at Sea (12 August 1949), Art. 48 [Geneva Convention II]; Geneva Convention relative to the Treatment of Prisoners of War (12 August 1949), Art. 127 [Geneva Convention III]; Geneva Convention relative to the Protection of Civilian Persons in Time of War (12 August 1949), Art. 144 [Geneva Convention IV] [together, Geneva Conventions of 1949]; Protocol Additional to the Geneva Conventions of 12 August 1949, and relating to the Protection of Victims of International Armed Conflicts (8 June 1977), Art. 83 [Additional Protocol I]; Protocol Additional to the Geneva Conventions of 12 August 1949, and relating to the Protection of Victims of Non-International Armed Conflicts (8 June 1977), Art. 19 [Additional Protocol II]. See also J.-M. Henckaerts & L. Doswald-Beck (eds.), *Customary International Humanitarian Law* (Cambridge and Geneva: Cambridge University Press and ICRC, 2005), Rules 142–143 [ICRC Customary IHL Study].

36 Additional Protocol I, *supra* note 35, Art. 56(7).

37 See, for example, A. Clapham, '*Focusing on armed non-state actors*', in A. Clapham & P. Gaeta, (eds.), *The Oxford Handbook of International Law in Armed Conflict* (Oxford: Oxford University Press, 2014) 766–810.

bear obligations under international human rights law remains controversial.[38] Accordingly, with a few exceptions, the Geneva List refers to the obligations of non-state actors stemming from international humanitarian law, duly noting the differences between parallel obligations applicable in international and non-international armed conflicts.

2 The Geneva List of Principles on the Protection of Water Infrastructure, with Commentaries[39]

2.1 *Principle 1: Objective and Scope*

1. The objective of the Geneva List is to ensure the protection of water infrastructure and water-related infrastructure during armed conflicts as well as to safeguard their utilization in post-conflict situations.
2. The Geneva List is intended for international and non-international armed conflicts as well as post-conflict situations.
3. The Geneva List is addressed to States and non-State actors.
4. The Geneva List is without prejudice to the applicable obligations of States and non-State actors under international law.

2.1.1 Commentary

1. The subject matter of the Geneva List is the protection of water infrastructure and water-related infrastructure.[40] To this end, the objectives of the List are twofold. First, it is to systematize the applicable international law rules to

38 See, for example, on the roles of non-state actors in international environmental law and international water law respectively, P. Sands & J. Peel, *Principles of International Environmental Law* (4th edition, Cambridge: Cambridge University Press, 2018) 89–96; K. Sangbana, '*The Role of Non-State Actors in the Development and Implementation of International Water Law*' in A. Rieu-Clarke, A. Allan & S. Hendry, *Routledge Handbook of Water Law and Policy* (London: Routledge, 2017) 287–296. See, for further on the obligations of non-state actors under international human rights law, A. Clapham, '*Non-state actors*', in D. Moeckli, S. Shah & S. Sivakumaran, *International Human Rights Law* (3rd edition, Oxford: Oxford University Press, 2018) 557–579; K. Fortin, *The Accountability of Armed Groups under Human Rights Law* (Oxford: Oxford University Press, 2017).

39 This version of the Geneva List of Principles and its Commentaries is dated April 2020 and contains corrections and updates to the version published in August 2019. The full list of principles without its commentary is reproduced in the Annex of this monograph.

40 The protection of water resources falls outside the scope of the Geneva List. However, Principle 15 on protection of the environment, refers to water resources as a component of the environment. For more on the protection of the environment, see ILC, *Protection of the Environment in Relation to Armed Conflict*, http://legal.un.org/ilc/guide/8_7.shtml, accessed 12 June 2020.

the protection of water infrastructure and water-related infrastructure during armed conflicts, as well as post-conflict periods. Second, it is to set forth the good practices and recommendations regarding their protection during these phases. Throughout the List, the terminology opted for aims at avoiding any confusion as to the nature of the principles, and doing so, any dilution of the strength of existing binding rules. For this purpose, the principles reflecting binding rules are drafted with 'must', and those which are non-binding good practices and recommendations with 'should', 'encouraged' or 'urged'.

2. The Geneva List is applicable to international and non-international armed conflicts alike. The differences in rules applicable to these two types of armed conflicts are reflected in the respective commentaries of the principles. The principles enshrined in the List concerning post-conflict situations are likewise applicable to contexts following both international and non-international armed conflicts. When a principle is also applicable in peacetime, prior to an armed conflict, it is set forth in the respective commentary. The principles reflecting the existing law are derived from treaty and customary law. They are based on, as applicable, instruments of international humanitarian law, international human rights law, international water law and international environmental law. The principles which consist of good practices and recommendations also take into account soft law documents.

3. The Geneva List is addressed to both states and non-state actors. The main non-state actor addressee of the List is non-state armed groups; nevertheless, other relevant actors, such as certain UN bodies, are considered as necessary. While the issue of the obligations of non-state actors under international human rights law, international environmental law and international water law remains unsettled, the existence of international humanitarian law of non-state armed groups is undisputed. The List takes note of the discussions on the issue without expanding on it and confines itself to clarifying the application of the respective principles to non-state when necessary.

4. The Geneva List does not alter or create binding obligations; states and non-state actors remain bound by their obligations stemming from treaties, customary law and other sources of international law, including unilateral declarations, which may go beyond the present principles.[41] It should be specified that during armed conflicts, the parties to the conflict may also conclude special agreements, undertaking further obligations than those provided by

41 For a list of declarations regarding water resources see, for example, Food and Agriculture Organization of the UN, *Systematic Index of International Water Resources Treaties, Declarations, Acts and Cases by Basin*, Legislative Study No. 15 (Rome: FAO, 1978).

international humanitarian law.[42] It is of note that the treaty law of international humanitarian law expressly encourages parties to conclude agreements on specific issues, such as the protection of works and installations containing dangerous forces.[43]

2.2 *Principle 2: Definitions*

For the purposes of the Geneva List:

(a) 'Water infrastructure' means all water and wastewater works, installations and facilities;

(b) 'Water-related infrastructure' means facilities, installations and other works which make an essential contribution to the functioning of water infrastructure so that their destruction or damage would render the water infrastructure inoperable.

2.2.1 Commentary

1. For the purposes of the Geneva List, the phrase 'water infrastructure' is used in a general manner, and it includes both water infrastructure and wastewater infrastructure. When looked at separately, water infrastructure consists of the components of the water supply systems and wastewater infrastructure consists of the components of wastewater collection, treatment and discharge or reuse systems. These include, but are not limited to, dams, dykes, water purification plants, desalination plants, water mills, water reservoirs, water towers, wells, pumping stations, sewerage systems, wastewater treatment plants, storage lagoons, transmission lines, conveyance lines and lifting stations. While mobile units, such as water tankers, used for water delivery where water infrastructure has been damaged or destroyed, do not necessarily fall within the scope of the List, they are referred to as necessary in the commentaries of the principles.

2. For the purposes of the Geneva List, 'water-related infrastructure' is used to include all infrastructure which generate and convey the energy required for the functioning of water infrastructure and all information and communications technology (ICT) infrastructure on which the water infrastructure relies for its operations. These include, but are not limited to, power plants such as electric generating stations, supply substations, transmission lines and distribution substations, along with the components of the ICT system. All such infrastructure, regardless of whether they are used solely for the powering of

42 Common Article 3 and Articles 6/6/6/7, respectively, of the four Geneva Conventions of 1949, *supra* note 35.

43 Additional Protocol I, *supra* note 35, Art. 56(6).

or operating water infrastructure or not, are within the scope of the List. The crucial common characteristic of these structures is their indispensability for the operation of water infrastructure in the provision of water for drinking, domestic uses, irrigation, along with the treatment of wastewater. Since their destruction or damaging lead to the cessation of water infrastructure's functioning, their protection is of great importance, in a way comparable to the integral parts of the water infrastructure per se.

3. The main functions of water infrastructure for the benefit of the population, in addition to the safe disposal of wastewater, can mainly be categorized according to four groups: provision of water for drinking; domestic uses; irrigation; and generating energy. The term should thus be understood to comprise all water structures, installations and facilities carrying out these functions, which, directly or indirectly, concern the health and survival of the population. It should be noted that water infrastructure is only one of the components of water services in general. Indeed, these services consist of three components: hardware (which includes infrastructure), consumables and people.[44] The latter two components are not the main focus of the Geneva List; however, rules concerning their protection are set forth as necessary, either in the body of the principles or in the text of the commentaries, with a view to ensuring a meaningful protection of water infrastructure.

2.3 *Principle 3: The Human Rights to Water and Sanitation*

> Everyone has the rights to water and sanitation, which are essential for the full enjoyment of all human rights.

2.3.1 Commentary

1. The human rights to water and sanitation are components of the right to an adequate standard of living,[45] and have been recognized as being indispens-

44 ICRC Urban Services Report, *supra* note 6, at 8 and 18: 'All urban services require three elements in order to function: people (i.e. service provider staff, private-sector contractors and entrepreneurs), hardware (e.g. infrastructure, equipment, heavy machinery) and consumables (e.g. fuel, chlorine, medicines)'.

45 United Nations Human Rights Council, '*Human rights and access to safe drinking water and sanitation*', 6 October 2010, UNHRC Resolution 15/9, UN Doc. A/HRC/RES/15/9, para 3. See also UN Committee on Economic, Social and Cultural Rights, 'General Comment No. 15: The right to water (Arts 11 and 12 of the Covenant)' (2003), para 3. The right to an adequate standard of living is stipulated in Article 11 of the International Covenant on Economic, Social and Cultural Rights (16 December 1966) [ICESCR].

able for the full enjoyment of all human rights, including the right to life.[46] It has been also set forth that these rights are 'inextricably related to the right to the highest attainable standard of physical and mental health',[47] and that the fulfilment of the right to water is also a requisite for the realization of the right to adequate food.[48] Acknowledging that the two rights are inherently linked, in line with the recent UN practice, the Geneva List treats them as two distinct rights.[49]

2. The human rights to water and sanitation entail obligations relating to both access to and the quality of the services. Indeed, the right to water requires that everyone has 'access to sufficient, safe, acceptable, physically accessible and affordable water for personal and domestic use'.[50] Likewise, the right to sanitation requires that everyone has 'physical and affordable access to sanitation, in all spheres of life, that is safe, hygienic, secure, socially and culturally acceptable'.[51]

---

46 United Nations General Assembly, '*The human rights to safe drinking water and sanitation*', 17 December 2015, UNGA Resolution 70/169, UN Doc. A/RES/70/169, para 1. The rights to water and sanitation are also included in other instruments: Convention on the Elimination of All Forms of Discrimination Against Women (18 December 1979), Art. 14(2)(h); Convention on the Rights of the Child (20 November 1989), Art. 24(2)(c) and (e); Convention on the Rights of Persons with Disabilities (13 December 2006), Art. 28(2)(a).

47 UNHRC Resolution 15/9, *supra* note 45, para 3. See also General Comment No. 15, *supra* note 45, para 3.

48 General Comment No. 15, *supra* note 45, para 7. See also UN Commission on Human Rights, *The Right to Food, Report submitted by the Special Rapporteur on the Right to Food, Jean Ziegler, in accordance with Commission on Human Rights Resolution 2002/25*, Doc E/CN.4/2003/54 (10 January 2003), at 13–17. Further, the former Special Rapporteur on the human rights to safe drinking water and sanitation noted the linkage between the rights to water and sanitation and other human rights such as education, privacy and the prohibition of cruel, inhumane or degrading treatment. See UN Human Rights Council, *Report of the Special Rapporteur on the Human Rights to Safe Drinking Water and Sanitation, Catarina de Albuquerque, Stigma and the Realization of the Human Rights to Water and Sanitation*, UN Doc A/HRC/21/42 (2 July 2012).

49 UNGA Resolution 70/169, *supra* note 46. See also United Nations Human Rights Council, '*The human rights to safe drinking water and sanitation*', 5 October 2018, UNHRC Resolution 39/8, UN Doc. A/HRC/RES/39/8, para 4: 'Also reaffirms that the human rights to safe drinking water and sanitation are interrelated, but have features that warrant distinct treatment in order to address specific challenges in their implementation'.

50 United Nations General Assembly, '*The human rights to safe drinking water and sanitation*'. 19 December 2017, UNGA Resolution 72/178, UN Doc. A/RES/72/178, para 2; General Comment No. 15, *supra* note 45, para 2. See also para 12 (a): '[Personal and domestic] uses ordinarily include drinking, personal sanitation, washing of clothes, food preparation, personal and household hygiene'.

51 UNGA Resolution 72/178, *supra* note 50, para 2.

3. The human rights to water and sanitation are informed by the principle of non-discrimination and equality as enshrined in Articles 2 and 3 of the International Covenant on Economic, Social and Cultural Rights.[52] Nevertheless, it is reported that certain groups, such as indigenous peoples, are commonly disadvantaged in access to water and sanitation.[53] Furthermore, the disadvantages in accessing water and sanitation are aggravated and consequent risks of violations of other human rights increased for certain groups, such as women and children, in times of armed conflict.[54]

4. In addition to its discriminatory effects on the more vulnerable groups of society, armed conflicts can also indiscriminately hinder people's access to water and sanitation services.[55] In turn, this lack of access can cause or worsen the other devastating effects of armed conflict, such as malnutrition and spread of diseases.[56] For example, UNICEF has reported that, on average, children under 5 are nearly 20 times more likely to die from diarrhoeal disease linked to unsafe water and sanitation facilities and lack of hygiene than violence during armed conflicts.[57]

52 UN Committee on Economic, Social and Cultural Rights, 'General Comment No. 20: Non-discrimination in economic, social and cultural rights (art. 2, para 2, of the International Covenant on Economic, Social and Cultural Rights)' (2009), paras 2 and 7; General Comment No. 15, *supra* note 45, paras 13–16. See also UNGA Resolution 70/169, *supra* note 46, para 2.

53 See UN Water, *Eliminating Discrimination and Inequalities in Access to Water and Sanitation*, Policy Brief (Geneva: UN Water, 2015), at 10–15.

54 See, for example, C. Lindsey-Curtet, F. Tercier Holst-Roness & L. Anderson, *Addressing the Needs of Women Affected by Armed Conflict: An ICRC Guidance Document* (Geneva: ICRC, 2004), at 57, 83; UN Department of Economic and Social Affairs, *A Gender Perspective on Water Resources and Sanitation*, Background Paper No. 2 UN Doc DESA/DSD/2005/2 (2005), at 17–18. See also UNICEF, Water Under Fire, *supra* note 9.

55 See UNGA Resolution 72/178, *supra* note 50, Preamble: 'Deeply concerned also about the lack of access to adequate water and sanitation services and its dramatic consequences for the overall health situation in humanitarian crises, including in times of conflict and natural disaster, acknowledging that people living in countries affected by conflict, violence and instability are four times as likely to lack basic drinking water and twice as likely to lack basic sanitation as people living in unaffected countries'.

56 See, for example, UN Office of the High Commissioner for Human Rights, 'Information Received Concerning the Negative Impact on the Enjoyment of Human Rights and the Apparent Blockage of Aircraft and Vessels Carrying Essential Goods from Entering Yemen' (17 November 2016), at 5: 'It is reported that two-thirds of Yemen's population do not have access to clean water supply. The lack of safe drinking water forces people to drink and use untreated water for cooking and personal use, and increases the chance of getting diarrhoea and other water-borne diseases. This situation mainly affects children and women, who are subjected to long distance travel to fetch water'.

57 UNICEF, *Water Under Fire* (21 March 2019), https://www.unicef.org/stories/water-under-fire, accessed 12 June 2020.

5. As stated by the Committee on Economic, Social and Cultural Rights, during armed conflicts, states must refrain from 'limiting access to, or destroying, water services and infrastructure as a punitive measure' in violation of international humanitarian law.[58] The Third and Fourth Geneva Conventions set forth specific obligations for Detaining Powers regarding access to water and sanitation by prisoners of war and civilian internees and Additional Protocol II does the same for persons deprived of their liberty for reasons related to non-international armed conflicts.[59] Occupying Powers also have specific obligations in ensuring and maintaining public health and hygiene services and preventing the spread of contagious diseases and epidemics.[60] Furthermore, in addition to the general rules on the conduct of hostilities, international humanitarian law prohibits the use of starvation of the civilian population as a method of warfare and grants specific protection to the objects indispensable for the survival of the civilian population both in international and non-international armed conflicts.[61] A failure in the protection of these objects can result in violations of both international humanitarian law and the rights to water and sanitation under international human rights law.

2.4 *Principle 4: Use of Water Infrastructure and Water-Related Infrastructure as a Means of Warfare*

1. The parties to the conflict should refrain from using water infrastructure and water-related infrastructure as a means of warfare.
2. In cases where water infrastructure and water-related infrastructure are used as a means of warfare during the conduct of hostilities, the principles of distinction, proportionality and precautions must be respected.

2.4.1 Commentary

1. Means of warfare include 'weapons in the widest sense' and methods of warfare are the ways, such as tactics or strategies, in which the means are used.[62]

---

58 General Comment No. 15, *supra* note 45, para 21. See also para 22: 'The Committee notes that during armed conflicts ... the right to water embraces those obligations by which States parties are bound under international humanitarian law'.

59 Geneva Convention III, *supra* note 35, Arts 20, 22, 26, 29, 46, 97; Geneva Convention IV, *supra* note 35, Arts 36, 49, 56, 76, 85, 89, 124, 127; Additional Protocol II, *supra* note 35, Art. 5. See also ICRC Customary IHL Study, *supra* note 35, Rule 118.

60 Geneva Convention IV, *supra* note 35, Art. 56. See Principle 18 on occupation.

61 Additional Protocol I, *supra* note 35, Art. 54; Additional Protocol II, *supra* note 35, Art. 14. See also ICRC Customary IHL Study, *supra* note 35, Rules 53–54. See Principle 12 on starvation and water infrastructure indispensable to the survival of the civilian population.

62 ICRC Commentary, *supra* note 1, para 1402. See also para 1401: 'The Conference preferred the term "methods and means of warfare" to the term "methods and means of combat",

Water infrastructure can be, and have been, utilized as a means of warfare during armed conflicts. Specifically, the parties to the conflict who have control over water infrastructure, such as dams, have resorted to flooding as a method of warfare, releasing water in high volumes. The consequences of these acts are severe and in most cases long-lasting; they include degradation of agricultural lands and displacement of civilians.[63] Water infrastructure has also been employed as a tool in warfare, in the ordinary meaning; the parties to the conflict have abused their control over this infrastructure to retain water, both for drinking and for irrigation, and to poison or otherwise alter the quality of the water retained.[64]

2. The use of water infrastructure, and water itself, in the context of armed conflict has been addressed by the ILA in the Madrid Rules of 1976. The Rules set forth two specific prohibitions for the protection of the civilian population and the environment:

a) The diversion of waters for military purposes should be prohibited when it would cause disproportionate suffering to the civilian population or substantial damage to the ecological balance of the area concerned. A diversion that is carried out in order to damage or destroy the minimum conditions of survival of the civilian population or the basic ecological balance of the area concerned or in order to terrorize the population should be prohibited in any case.[65]

b) The causing of floods as well as any other interference with the hydrologic balance ... should be prohibited when it involves grave dangers to the civilian population or substantial damage to the ecological balance of the area concerned.[66]

3. During the drafting of the UN Watercourses Convention, it was proposed by the Special Rapporteur at the time to include provisions on employment of

---

which was used in the ICRC draft, "for the reason that 'combat' might be construed more narrowly than 'warfare'." It is clear that the term "warfare" encompasses "combat", a term that is used occasionally in the Protocol' (footnotes omitted).

63 See T. von Lossow, '*The Rebirth of Water as a Weapon: IS in Syria and Iraq*', 51:3, The International Spectator (2016) 82–99, at 88.

64 See *Id.*, p. 87: 'There are essentially three main ways to use water as a weapon, namely by making sure that there is either too little, or alternatively too much water—both of which involve manipulating quantity—or that water is unusable, by reducing its quality' (footnotes omitted). See also Principles 5, 12 and 14 on poison and poisoned weapons, starvation and water infrastructure indispensable to the survival of the civilian population and acts or threats the primary purpose of which is to spread terror among the civilian population respectively.

65 Madrid Rules, *supra* note 32, Art. 3.

66 *Id.*, Art. 5.

water and water infrastructure as means of warfare. Even though these proposals were later excluded from the draft convention, the following paragraphs of the draft Article 13 are noteworthy:

> 3. Hydraulic installations and other facilities, associated with an international watercourse system and capable of releasing dangerous forces or substances, shall not be used in preparation for, or in the conduct of, offensive military operations.
>
> 6. Withholding, by diversion or other means, of water from a system State so as to place in jeopardy the survival of the civilian population or to imperil the viability of the environment is prohibited in peacetime and in time of armed conflict.[67]

4. The use of water infrastructure as a means of warfare is not specifically regulated by international humanitarian law; however, during armed conflicts, the right of the parties to the conflict to choose methods and means of warfare is not unlimited.[68] This basic rule stems from the balance between the principles of humanity and military necessity on which international humanitarian law is based.[69] The considerations of military necessity allow the parties to the conflict to take measures necessary to weaken and defeat the opposing party's armed forces. On the other hand, the considerations of humanity set a limit to these allowed measures by, for example, imposing that the parties to a conflict do not cause superfluous injury and unnecessary suffering or widespread, long-term and severe damage to the natural environment.[70] The parties to the conflict must carefully analyse this equilibrium in instances where the use of water infrastructure as a means of warfare is considered, both in international and non-international armed conflicts. In any case, they must comply with the principles of distinction, proportionality and precautions in the conduct of hostilities.[71]

67 ILC, *Third Report on the Law of the Non-navigational Uses of International Watercourses, by Mr. Stephen M. Schwebel, Special Rapporteur*, Doc A/CN.4/348 (11 December 1981), at 169.

68 Additional Protocol I, *supra* note 35, Art. 35(1).

69 ICRC Commentary, *supra* note 1, para 1389: 'The law of armed conflict is a compromise based on a balance between military necessity, on the one hand, and the requirements of humanity, on the other'. See also ICRC Customary IHL Study, *supra* note 35, Commentary to Rule 70.

70 Additional Protocol I, *supra* note 35, Art. 35(2)–(3); ICRC Customary IHL Study, *supra* note 35, Rules 45 and 70.

71 These principles are dealt with in Principles 6 to 11 on principles on conduct of hostilities.

2.5 *Principle 5: Poison or Poisoned Weapons*

The use of poison or poisoned weapons against water and water infrastructure is prohibited.

2.5.1 Commentary

1. The prohibition of using poison as a weapon has been in force since the Hague Convention II.[72] This rule is part of customary international law applicable to international and non-international armed conflicts.[73] This prohibition is also included in some soft law documents of international water law[74] and incorporated by several states in their military manuals.[75] At least one military

72 Hague Convention (II) with respect to the Laws and Customs of war on Land and its Annex: Regulations concerning the Laws and Customs of War on Land (29 July 1899), Art. 23(a) [Hague Convention II]. This prohibition was reproduced in the Hague Convention (IV) Respecting the Laws and Customs of War on Land and its Annex: Regulations Concerning the Laws and Customs of War on Land (18 October 1907), Annexed Regulations, Art. 23(a) [Hague Regulations]. These regulations are accepted as reflecting customary international law. See Nuremberg International Military Tribunal, *Trial of the Major War Criminals, 14 November 1945–1 October 1946*, Nuremberg, 1947, Vol. 1, at 253–254; ICJ, Legality of the Threat or Use of Nuclear Weapons, Advisory Opinion, 8 July 1996, paras 80–82 [Nuclear Weapons Advisory Opinion]. It should be noted that prior to the Hague Convention II, this prohibition was already set forth in some national documents (see, for example, Instructions for the Government of Armies of the United States in the Field (Lieber Code) (24 April 1863), Arts. 16, 70). While this rule has been in force a long time, there are still reports of poisoning of water during armed conflicts. See, for example, T. von Lossow, '*Water as Weapon: IS on the Euphrates and Tigris*', SWP Comments 3 (Berlin: German Institute for International and Security Studies, 2016), at 2, https://www.swp-berlin.org/fileadmin/contents/products/comments/2016C03_lsw.pdf, accessed 12 June 2020: 'In December 2014, IS deliberately contaminated drinking water with crude oil in the Balad district of Salahaddin Governorate, south of Tikrit. There were also reports of poisoned water supplies from Aleppo, Deir ez-Zor, Raqqa and Baghdad'.

73 ICRC Customary IHL Study, *supra* note 35, Rule 72.

74 Madrid Rules, *supra* note 32, Art. 1; Berlin Rules, *supra* note 32, Art. 50. See also a draft Article 13(1) of the UN Watercourses Convention, which was later omitted: 'System States shall employ their best efforts to prevent the poisoning of shared water resources by any and all persons or from any source'. ILC, *supra* note 67, at 169.

75 ICRC Customary IHL Study, *supra* note 35, Commentary to Rule 72. See, for example, Germany, *Humanitarian Law in Armed Conflicts—Manual*, DSK VV207320067, The Federal Ministry of Defence of the Federal Republic of Germany, VR II 3 (August 1992), English translation of ZDv 15/2, paras. 426 and 434: 'The prohibition [of poison and poisoned weapons] also applies to the toxic contamination of water supply installations and foodstuffs ... for military purposes.'; Australia, *Law of Armed Conflict*, Australian Defence Doctrine Publication 06.4 (11 May 2006) [Australia Manual], para 4.8: '[T]he poisoning or contamination of any source of drinking water is prohibited and the illegality is not cured by posting a notice that the water has been so contaminated or poisoned'.

manual specifically mentions different types of water infrastructure necessary for access to drinking water.[76]

2. The terms 'poison' or 'poisoned weapons' are not defined in the international instruments regulating their use. As explained by the International Court of Justice (ICJ), they have been understood in state practice 'in their ordinary sense as covering weapons whose prime, or even exclusive, effect is to poison or asphyxiate'.[77] Regarding the question of incidental poisoning, some states clearly set out in their written statements in the Nuclear Weapons Advisory Opinion that the prohibition does extend to these incidents.[78] Others, on the other hand, set forth in their written statements that the use of nuclear weapons would be illegal due to their poisonous, even if not intended, effects.[79] The legality of the use of weapons which are not specifically designed to be poisonous but which have secondary poisonous effects remains at best unsettled. Consequently, the prohibition as it stands today does not necessarily encompass incidental poisoning. On the other hand, the Geneva List holds even under this interpretation, because the prohibition covers, for example, targeting of

76 United Kingdom, *The Law of War on Land being Part III of the Manual of Military Law* (The War Office, 1958), paras 111–112: 'Water in wells, pumps, pipes, reservoirs, lakes, rivers and the like, from which the enemy may draw drinking water, must not be poisoned or contaminated'.

77 Nuclear Weapons Advisory Opinion, *supra* note 72, para 55.

78 Written statement of the United Kingdom (16 June 1995), Legality of the Threat or Use of Nuclear Weapons (Advisory Opinion), para 3.60: 'The prohibitions in both Article 23(a) of the Hague Regulations and the 1925 Protocol were, however, intended to apply to weapons whose primary effect was poisonous and not to those where poison was a secondary or incidental effect.'; Written statement of the United States of America (20 June 1995), Legality of the Threat or Use of Nuclear Weapons (Advisory Opinion), at 24: 'This prohibition [on the use of poison weapons] was established with particular reference to projectiles that carry poison into the body of the victim. It was not intended to apply, and has not been applied, to weapons that are designed to injure or cause destruction by other means, even though they also may create toxic byproducts'. According to the ICRC Customary IHL Study, '[t]his interpretation does not indicate that poison must be the primary or exclusive injury mechanism but that it must be an "intended" injury mechanism' (ICRC Customary IHL Study, *supra* note 35, Commentary to Rule 72).

79 Written statement of Sweden (20 June 1995), Legality of the Threat or Use of Nuclear Weapons (Advisory Opinion), at 5: 'As far back as the 17th century, Hugo Grotius stressed that poisoning was not allowed under international law. In certain respects, the principle of the prohibition of toxic weapons has also been codified (chiefly as a result of the 1925 Geneva Convention). Certain residual products resulting from the use of nuclear weapons must undoubtedly be regarded as toxic.'; Written statement of the Marshall Islands (22 June 1995), Legality of the Threat or Use of Nuclear Weapons (Advisory Opinion), at 3–4: 'Additionally, any use of nuclear weapons violate laws of war including the Geneva and Hague Conventions and the United Nations Charter. Such laws prohibit the use of poisonous substances'.

hazardous facilities with an intent to poison a nearby water source. It should be added that, in any case, targeting a hazardous facility would be in violation of international humanitarian law, as its effects cannot be limited as required by the rules on conduct of hostilities.[80]

3. Altering the state of water not amounting to poisoning is outside the scope of this principle. However, it should be noted that this issue is dealt with by the Madrid and Berlin Rules adopted by the ILA; both documents prohibit rendering water which is indispensable for the health and survival of the civilian population unfit for human consumption.[81] Moreover, according to the definition of the human right to water, 'water for personal or domestic use must be safe, therefore free from micro-organisms, chemical substances and radiological hazards that constitute a threat to a person's health'.[82]

4. In cases where the poisoning has transboundary effects, a violation of the obligation not to cause transboundary harm as established under international environmental law can also come into question.[83] The UN Watercourses Convention, the ILC Draft Articles on Aquifers and the UNECE Convention all codify the obligation not to cause significant transboundary harm.[84] When significant harm is nevertheless caused, the state causing the harm has the

80 Additional Protocol I, *supra* note 35, Art. 51(4). See also on the intrinsic indiscriminate character of poisoning as a method of warfare, ICRC Commentary, *supra* note 1, para 1963: 'There are also methods which by their very nature have an indiscriminate character, such as poisoning wells'. See Principle 8 on indiscriminate attacks.

81 Madrid Rules, *supra* note 32, Art. 1; Berlin Rules, *supra* note 32, Commentary to Article 50: 'Civilians are entitled to an adequate water supply under all circumstances. Hence the prohibition of any action, whatever the motive, which would have the effect of denying the civilian population of the necessary water supply. The rule has been expanded to protect all vital human needs, a concept that in these Rules means water necessary to assure human health and survival'.

82 General Comment No. 15, *supra* note 45, para 12(b). In this context, the World Health Organization's (WHO) Guidelines for Drinking Water Quality represent an authoritative document to determine the safety of water supplies. See WHO, *Guidelines for Drinking Water Quality: Fourth edition incorporating the first addendum* (Geneva: WHO, 2017). These Guidelines have already been used in the context of occupied territories (see, for example, UNICEF, *Protecting Children from Unsafe Water in Gaza: Strategy, Action Plan and Project Resources* (UNICEF, 2011)).

83 Nuclear Weapons Advisory Opinion, *supra* note 72, para 29.

84 Convention on the Law of Non-navigational Uses of International Watercourses (21 May 1997), Art. 7 [UN Watercourses Convention]; International Law Commission (ILC), '*Draft Articles on the Law of Transboundary Aquifers, with Commentaries*', II:Part II, Yearbook of the International Law Commission (2008), 19–43, Art. 6 [ILC Draft Articles on Aquifers]; Convention on the Protection of Transboundary Watercourses and International Lakes (17 March 1992), Art. 2 [UNECE Convention].

obligation to take, in consultation with the affected states, all appropriate means to eliminate or mitigate such harm.[85]

2.6 *Principle 6: Attacks against Water Infrastructure and Water-Related Infrastructure*

Water infrastructure and water-related infrastructure are presumed to be civilian objects and, in such case, must not be attacked.

2.6.1 Commentary

1. Civilian objects are protected against attacks. The prohibition of attacks against civilian objects is based on the principle of distinction as codified in Article 48 of Additional Protocol I, which stipulates that 'the Parties to the conflict shall at all times distinguish between ... civilian objects and military objectives and accordingly shall direct their operations only against military objectives'.[86] This rule is part of customary international law applicable to international and non-international armed conflicts.[87]

2. Civilian objects are defined in a negative manner as 'all objects which are not military objectives'.[88] There is no third category of objects.[89] Objects that are of 'dual-use', both military and civilian, must not be made the object of

85 UN Watercourses Convention, *supra* note 84, Arts 7, 27, 28; ILC Draft Articles on Aquifers, *supra* note 84, Arts 6, 17.

86 Additional Protocol I, *supra* note 35, Art. 48. See also Article 52(2): 'Attacks shall be limited strictly to military objectives'. This rule constitutes the foundational principle of international humanitarian law and was recognized as early as 1868 in the St. Petersburg Declaration. Its Preamble states that 'the only legitimate object which States should endeavour to accomplish during war is to weaken the military forces of the enemy'. See Declaration Renouncing the Use, in Time of War, of Explosive Projectiles Under 400 Grammes Weight (11 December 1868).

87 ICRC Customary IHL Study, *supra* note 35, Rules 7 and 10. See also Nuclear Weapons Advisory Opinion, *supra* note 72, paras 78–79.

88 Additional Protocol I, *supra* note 35, Art. 52(1); ICRC Customary IHL Study, *supra* note 35, Rule 9. The definition of military objectives is contextual; they are 'those objects which by their nature, location, purpose or use make an effective contribution to military action and whose total or partial destruction, capture or neutralization, in the circumstances ruling at the time, offers a definite military advantage'. See Additional Protocol I, *supra* note 35, Art. 52(2); ICRC Customary IHL Study, *supra* note 35, Rule 8.

89 M. N. Schmitt (ed.), *Tallinn Manual 2.0 on the International Law Applicable to Cyber Operations* (Cambridge: Cambridge University Press, 2017), at 445, Commentary to Rule 101, para 1; United States, Department of Defense, *Law of War Manual* (June 2015, updated December 2016), para 5.6.1.2. See also ICRC Customary IHL Study, *supra* note 35, Commentary to Rule 9: '[O]nly those objects that qualify as military objectives may be attacked; other objects are protected against attack'.

attacks if they do not meet the definition of military objectives at the time of the attack.[90] In case of doubt as to whether an object that is normally dedicated to civilian purposes is being used to make an effective contribution to military action, it must be presumed not to be so used.[91]

3. Water infrastructure and water-related infrastructure are presumed to be used for civilian purposes; they are civilian objects and must not be deliberately targeted.[92] However, in certain situations they may be considered to make an effective contribution to military action. According to the definition of military objectives, this contribution should be made by the nature, location, purpose or use of the object. It should first be noted that a water infrastructure does not and cannot by nature contribute to military action;[93] in fact, it can constitute military objectives only in strictly limited instances. For example, a water pumping station that provides water both to a town and military barracks or a river dam used for military transport, in addition to providing irrigation water to nearby villages can be considered to be military objectives due to their use.[94]

90 The term 'dual-use' does not have any legal significance and is used here only for practical purposes.

91 Additional Protocol I, *supra* note 35, Art. 52(3); ICRC Customary IHL Study, *supra* note 35, Commentary to Rule 10; Canada, *Use of Force for CF Operations*, Canadian Forces Joint Publication, B-GJ-005-501/FP-001 (August 2008), para 112.3; France, *Manuel de droit des conflits armés* (Ministère de la Défense, 2001), at 90; United Kingdom, *The Manual of the Law of Armed Conflict* (Ministry of Defence, 1 July 2004), para 5.24.3 [UK Manual].

92 See UK Manual (2004), *supra* note 91, para 5.24.2: '[The term 'civilian objects'] also includes foodstuffs and food producing areas, springs, wells, water works and other water sources, buildings, and facilities used by civilians (so long as they do not fall within the definition of military objectives).'; Israel Ministry of Foreign Affairs, 'Preserving Humanitarian Principles While Combating Terrorism: Israel's Struggle with Hezbollah in the Lebanon War', Diplomatic Notes No. 1 (April 2007), at 5: 'Significant damage was also inflicted on infrastructure: sewage plants were damaged and, in some cases, sewage had to be released into the sea and atmosphere (by burning).... All these clearly constitute civilian objects, which are protected from attack by international law, and whose destruction served no military purpose whatsoever'; and at 15: 'The guiding principle adopted by the [Israel Defense Forces] was to target only infrastructure that was making a significant contribution to the operational capabilities of the Hezbollah terrorists. This meant that, for the most part, Israeli attacks were limited to the transportation infrastructure. Most of the other infrastructure (medical, cultural, railroad, tunnels, ports, banking, manufacturing, farming, tourism, sewage, financial, electricity, drainage, water and the like) was left almost completely untouched'.

93 According to the ICRC Commentary, *supra* note 1, para 2020, '[t]his category [of military objectives by nature] comprises all objects directly used by the armed forces'.

94 In the case of the water pumping station providing water both to a town and military barracks, the principle of precautions would require the attacking party, if possible, to hit, for example, the pipe leading to the barracks from the pumping station in a place where it would cut water only to military barracks and not civilians.

Even when it can be established that water infrastructure meets the definition of a military objective, it will in most cases also have a civilian use and its targeting will have far-reaching consequences on the civilian population. In these cases, attacks against water infrastructure are governed by the principles of proportionality and precautions.[95] More importantly, some water infrastructure cannot be targeted even when it is established that they are military objectives.[96]

2.7 *Principle 7: Attacks against the Personnel Working for Water Infrastructure and Water-Related Infrastructure*

> Personnel responsible for carrying out tasks related to the operation, maintenance, assessment, repair and rehabilitation of water infrastructure and water-related infrastructure are presumed to be civilians and, in such case, must not be attacked.

2.7.1 Commentary

1. Civilians must not be made the objects of attacks. The prohibition of attacks against civilians is based on the principle of distinction as codified in Article 48 of Additional Protocol I, which stipulates that 'the Parties to the conflict shall at all times distinguish between the civilian population and combatants'.[97] Consequently, '[t]he civilian population as such, as well as individual civilians, shall not be made the object of attack'.[98] This rule is part of customary international law applicable to international and non-international armed conflicts.[99]

2. Civilians working for or at the water infrastructure or water-related infrastructure, including but not necessarily limited to engineers, technical staff, operators, repair and construction crews, administrative staff and other personnel, must be protected against attack unless and for such time as they take a direct part in hostilities.[100] The same rule applies to the personnel of civil

95 See Principles 9 and 10 on proportionality in attack and precautions in attack respectively.

96 See Principles 12 and 13 on starvation and water infrastructure indispensable to the survival of the civilian population water infrastructure containing dangerous forces.

97 Additional Protocol I, *supra* note 35, Art. 48.

98 *Id.*, Art. 51(2); Additional Protocol II, *supra* note 35, Art. 13(2).

99 ICRC Customary IHL Study, *supra* note 35, Rules 1 and 6; Nuclear Weapons Advisory Opinion, *supra* note 72, paras 78–79.

100 Additional Protocol I, *supra* note 35, Art. 51(3); ICRC Customary IHL Study, *supra* note 35, Rule 6. See for further on the notion of direct participation in hostilities, N. Melzer, *Interpretive Guidance on the Notion of Direct Participation in Hostilities under International Humanitarian Law* (Geneva: ICRC, 2009). The activities set forth in the principle do not constitute direct participation in hostilities.

defence and humanitarian organizations involved in the operation, maintenance, assessment, repair and rehabilitation of water infrastructure and water-related infrastructure.[101] Regarding dams and dykes specifically, people employed as guards for the sole purpose of defending the protected works or installations are also protected from attack, provided that they are not used in hostilities.[102] In case of doubt as to the civilian character of a person working for or at water infrastructure or water-related infrastructure, the person must be presumed to be a civilian.[103]

2.8 *Principle 8: Indiscriminate Attacks*

> Attacks which do not or cannot distinguish between military objectives and civilian objects, including water infrastructure and water-related infrastructure, are prohibited.

2.8.1 Commentary

1. The prohibition of indiscriminate attacks is codified in Additional Protocol I and is part of customary international law applicable to international and non-international armed conflicts.[104] This Principle stems from the principle of distinction, but is different from the rules set forth in Principles 6 and 7, which concern intentional targeting of civilian objects and civilians respectively. The present Principle sets forth the prohibition of attacks which are of a nature to strike military objectives and civilians or civilian objects without distinction. Indiscriminate attacks are those which (a) are not directed at a specific military objective or, (b) because of the method or means that is employed cannot be directed at a specific military objective or, (c) attacks the effects of which cannot be limited as required by international humanitarian law, due to the choice of method or means.[105]

---

101 See also Principle 17 on humanitarian access and assistance.

102 Additional Protocol I, *supra* note 35, Art. 56(5): '[I]nstallations erected for the sole purpose of defending the protected works or installations from attack are permissible and shall not themselves be made the object of attack, provided that they are not used in hostilities except for defensive actions necessary to respond to attacks against the protected works or installations and that their armament is limited to weapons capable only of repelling hostile action against the protected works or installations'.

103 *Id.*, Art. 50(1); ICRC Customary IHL Study, *supra* note 35, Commentary to Rule 6.

104 Additional Protocol I, *supra* note 35, Art. 51(4); ICRC Customary IHL Study, *supra* note 35, Rule 11.

105 Additional Protocol I, *supra* note 35, Art. 51(4); ICRC Customary IHL Study, *supra* note 35, Rule 12.

2. Water infrastructure and water-related infrastructure in densely populated areas, especially in urban warfare contexts, are especially vulnerable against indiscriminate attacks, even if they are not directly targeted themselves.[106] The use of explosive weapons in these contexts indiscriminately hit both military objectives and civilian objects, including water infrastructure providing drinking water to the civilian population. Their use should be avoided in densely populated areas to ensure the full protection of the civilian population and water infrastructure and water-related infrastructure that they depend on.[107]

2.9 *Principle 9: Proportionality in Attack*

1. Attacks against water infrastructure and water-related infrastructure, when these are military objectives, which may be expected to cause incidental loss of civilian life, injury to civilians, damage to civilian objects, or a combination thereof, which would be excessive in relation to the concrete and direct military advantage anticipated, are prohibited.
2. Attacks against military objectives which may be expected to cause incidental loss of civilian life, injury to civilians, damage to civilian objects, including water infrastructure and water-related infrastructure, or a combination thereof, which would be excessive in relation to the concrete and direct military advantage anticipated, are prohibited.
3. The reverberating, or indirect, effects that are foreseeable in the circumstances at the time of the attack should be taken into account in the assessment of proportionality.

106 For the purposes of international humanitarian law, a densely populated area 'should be understood as synonymous with "concentration of civilians", defined in international humanitarian law as "a city, town, village or other area containing a similar concentration of civilians or civilian objects".' ICRC, '*Explosive Weapons in Populated Areas*', Factsheet (2016).

107 ICRC, *International Humanitarian Law and the Challenges of Contemporary Armed Conflicts*, Doc 32IC/15/11 (October 2015), at 49 [ICRC Challenges Report]. There is growing concern about the use of explosive weapons in populated areas also in state practice. See, for example, Ambassador Geraldine Byrne Nason, 'Joint Statement on Explosive Weapons in Populated Areas (EWIPA)', UNGA 73 (25 October 2018) (on behalf of 50 states). Significantly, the Joint Statement affirms that '[t]he use of explosive weapons in populated areas has been shown to cause long-term humanitarian harm, which far outlasts the conflicts in which they are used. Beyond the immediate injuries and deaths caused, the destruction of housing, schools, hospitals, water and sanitation systems and other crucial infrastructure means that the civilian population is severely affected over the long term' (para 4).

2.9.1 Commentary

1. The principle of proportionality is codified in Additional Protocol I and is part of customary international law applicable to international and non-international armed conflicts.[108] The concept of proportionality is also addressed in documents of branches of international law other than international humanitarian law. For example, the ILA's Berlin Rules state that '[c]ombatants shall not, for military purposes or as reprisals ... destroy water installations, if such actions would cause disproportionate suffering to civilians'.[109]

2. The application of the principle of proportionality under international humanitarian law requires the exercise of balancing the concrete and direct military advantage anticipated from an attack with the expected civilian loss and damage to civilian objects, or a combination thereof.[110] In the case of water infrastructure and water-related infrastructure, the humanitarian consequences related to the access to water of the civilian population or necessary to the irrigation of lands providing food should weigh heavily, and, in the majority of the cases, surpass any anticipated military advantage.[111]

3. Attacks against water-related infrastructure, such as electrical facilities, can lead to the shutdown of water infrastructure and thus to the disruption of water distribution, agricultural irrigation and wastewater treatment, oftentimes resulting in indiscriminate effects. The assessment of proportionality carried out prior to the attack should include both the effects on the water infrastructure and the impacts caused by the disruption of services provided by them. Experience from past and current conflicts clearly demonstrates how the targeting of water infrastructure and water-related infrastructure may directly or indirectly affect the civilian population.[112] The effects of such

---

108 Additional Protocol I, *supra* note 35, Art. 51(5)(b); ICRC Customary IHL Study, *supra* note 35, Rule 14.

109 Berlin Rules, *supra* note 32, Art. 51(1).

110 The calculation of proportionality has proven to be a difficult exercise. See E.-C. Gillard, '*Proportionality in the Conduct of Hostilities: The Incidental Harm Side of the Assessment*', Research Paper (London: Chatham House, 2018), para 78: 'It requires valuing and comparing two incommensurable factors: military advantage and incidental harm'.

111 See also *Id.*, para 150: 'As far as facilities that provide services essential to the survival of the civilian population are concerned—such as medical facilities, electricity-generating and distribution networks, and water treatment systems—particular weight should be given to the damage to the installations themselves, in addition to including the deaths and injury expected from their destruction'.

112 See Gillard, *supra* note 110, para 168 regarding information to be gathered and taken into account in the assessment of attacks includes 'information in the public domain, information that can be acquired by the belligerents' intelligence-gathering systems, and information based on past practice'. See also para 171: 'Information on the harm that was actually caused can help estimate incidental harm more accurately for future

attacks cannot be claimed to be unexpected, and the lessons learnt in previous attacks should inform the assessment of proportionality.[113]

4. In the limited cases where it can be established that a water infrastructure is a military objective, the targeting of this infrastructure is governed by the principle of proportionality. Water infrastructure that can be characterized as military objectives would in most cases be 'dual-use' objects, that is, objects which have a military value but are also of importance to the civilian population.[114] Indeed, only in exceptional cases is water infrastructure dedicated solely to military use. A characteristic of water infrastructure which serves both civilian and military uses is that generally there is no clear boundary between these uses; this infrastructure most often continuously and in its entirety fulfils both civilian and military functions.[115] An example of 'dual-use' water infrastructure is a wastewater treatment plant that is also used as a depot for ammunition by the armed forces. In the absence of any possibility for separating the military use as an objective of attack, the attackers should take into account the consequent loss of or interference with the civilian use and apply the principle of proportionality in the strictest manner.[116] It should

---

attacks, and thus refine proportionality assessments'. See also Principle 10 on precautions in attack.

113 See, for example, L. Gisel (ed.), *The Principle of Proportionality in the Rules Governing the Conduct of Hostilities under International Humanitarian Law, International Expert Meeting Report, 22–23 June 2016, Quebec* (Geneva: International Committee of the Red Cross, 2018) [ICRC Proportionality Report], at 48: 'One expert recalled the example of the electricity cuts caused during the 1990–1991 Gulf War. Even if their impact was not fully foreseeable at the time, belligerents in subsequent conflicts could no longer claim that such an impact was hypothetical. It was noted that state practice had evolved: in the 2003 Gulf War the US-led coalition targeted switching stations instead of power stations, as the former are easier to repair than the latter and thus less likely to lead to long-lasting electricity cuts'.

114 ICRC Commentary, *supra* note 1, para 2023.

115 ICRC Proportionality Report, *supra* note 113, at 37.

116 See, for example, United States, Joint Chiefs of Staff, *Joint Targeting*, Joint publication 3-60 (31 January 2013), at A-5: 'If the attack is directed against dual-use objects that might be legitimate military targets but also serve a legitimate civilian need (e.g., electrical power or telecommunications), then this factor must be carefully balanced against the military benefits when making a proportionality determination'. (Referred to in the ICRC Proportionality Report, *supra* note 113, 39.) See also Gillard, *supra* note 110, para 127: 'There is general agreement that civilian deaths and injury and damage to civilian objects expected to occur as a result of the impairment of the continuing civilian function must be included in proportionality assessments'.

be noted that some water infrastructure has immunity against attacks under international humanitarian law, even when they have military functions.[117]

5. The targeting of certain water infrastructure can also lead to the deterioration of the environment, for example due to a leak of hazardous stored materials, such as a leak of chlorine following an attack against a water purification plant or pollution of the soil and water resources due to a targeting of a wastewater treatment plant. Today it is widely accepted that the environment is a civilian object and, consequently, any damage to it should be included in the proportionality assessment, whether this damage has effects on the civilian population or not.[118] Furthermore, any attacks which may be expected to cause widespread, long-term and severe damage to the environment are prohibited, regardless of whether it is excessive in relation to the expected military advantage.[119]

6. The reverberating, or indirect, effects of targeting water infrastructure and water-related infrastructure that are reasonably foreseeable under the circumstances at the time of the attack should be taken into account in the assessment of proportionality.[120] Indeed, it is of note that while the anticipated military advantage must be direct, there is no indication that the expected civilian harm should be as such.[121] Reverberating effects are the consequences of an attack which are not direct or are not manifest in the immediate aftermath

117 See Principles 12 and 13 on starvation and water infrastructure indispensable to the survival of the civilian population and water infrastructure containing dangerous forces respectively.

118 ICRC Customary IHL Study, *supra* note 35, Rule 43(c); International Institute of Humanitarian Law (L. Doswald-Beck (ed.)), *San Remo Manual on International Law Applicable to Armed Conflicts at Sea* (Cambridge and New York: Cambridge University Press, 1995), para 13(c). See also Gillard, *supra* note 110, paras 135–136.

119 Additional Protocol I, *supra* note 35, Arts 35(3), 55(1); ICRC Customary IHL Study, *supra* note 35, Rule 45. It should be noted that this customary rule is only arguably applicable to non-international armed conflicts. See also Principle 15 on protection of the environment.

120 ICRC Challenges Report, *supra* note 107, at 52; ICRC Proportionality Report, *supra* note 113, at 46. This is supported by state practice; for example, at least one military manual explicitly refers to indirect effects as 'factors involved in weighing anticipated incidental injuries/death to protected persons' (United States Navy, *The Commander's Handbook on the Law of Naval Operations* (August 2017), para 8.11.4). The Handbook gives as an example 'the anticipated incidental injury/death that may occur from disrupting an electric generating plant that supplies power to a military headquarters and to a hospital'.) See also Tallinn Manual 2.0, *supra* note 89, at 472, Commentary to Rule 113, para 6: 'The collateral damage considered in the proportionality calculation includes any indirect effects that should be expected by those individuals planning, approving, or executing a cyber attack'.

121 Gillard, *supra* note 110, paras 43 and 63.

of the attack.[122] These consequences are often heavier than the direct effects of an attack. For the purposes of the proportionality assessment under international humanitarian law, the temporal or spatial remoteness of the harm is irrelevant as long as it does not render the effects unforeseeable. Indeed, the determinative test here is reasonable foreseeability; the attacking party must take into account the reverberating effects that are reasonably foreseeable, based on the information reasonably available at the time of the attack.[123] Damage to water infrastructure and water-related infrastructure can cause, among others, a shortage of drinking water and of water necessary to the production of food and consequently can lead to the loss of more civilian lives than the attack itself. The reverberating effects of the disruption of water services include starvation, epidemics (especially water-borne diseases) and displacement, as well as deterioration of health services.[124] Consequently, the

122 See also *Id.*, para 61: 'Incidental harm can arise in a variety of ways. At its simplest, it can occur and manifest itself immediately upon an attack, as when shell fragments injure a civilian located in the proximity of a military objective. However, it can also occur immediately upon an attack but only manifest itself some time afterwards, as when toxic weapons cause disease that only becomes apparent months after the attack. Or it can occur long after the attack, as when a civilian is injured by unexploded cluster submunitions months or years after they were employed in an attack. The harm can occur in a single causal step, as in the examples above; or in a number of steps, as when an attack damages an object providing vital services to the civilian population, such as an electricity generation and distribution system, which in turn prevents water purification systems from operating, leading to an outbreak of waterborne diseases among the civilian population'.

123 *Id.*, paras 51–58. See also Principle 10 on precautions in attack.

124 See, for example, UN Human Rights Council, *Report of the Independent International Commission of Inquiry on the Syrian Arab Republic*, UN Doc A/HRC/34/64 (2 February 2017), para 26: 'Bombardment of water stations forced the population in the east to drink water from boreholes, risking the contraction of waterborne diseases'. See also ICRC, *Water and War: ICRC Response* (Geneva: ICRC, 2009), at 8: 'Access to water is frequently restricted because water supply or purification systems have been destroyed, because water reserves are located in areas that have become dangerous or because of massive displacement. People ultimately resort to sources of water with a high health risk. Many people contract water-borne diseases, thus placing even more pressure on under-equipped hospitals and dispensaries that are already hard put to cope with the influx of patients during the conflict'. See also, ICRC Urban Services Report, *supra* note 6, at 28: 'The quality of health services is dependent on potable water and a reliable power supply'. It should be noted that Article 51(5)(b) of Additional Protocol I, *supra* note 35, explicitly refers to loss of civilian life, and thus illnesses which eventually lead to death are clearly included in the proportionality. Diseases which do not lead to death, on the other hand, can be considered akin to injury to civilians, which is also foreseen in the provision as an element to be taken into account in the assessment of the proportionality of an attack. See also ICRC

calculation of proportionality should include the risk of any disease outbreaks, starvation, displacement[125] or environmental damage caused by the targeting or incidental damaging of water infrastructure.

7. The inclusion of reverberating effects in the proportionality assessment is especially significant in urban warfare contexts. The increasing interconnectivity of public services and thus their increasing vulnerability add to the complexity of the proportionality assessment.[126] The damaging or destruction of any infrastructure in these contexts is likely to have an adverse domino effect on other facilities that contribute to the provision of drinking water and water for domestic uses.[127]

8. The parties to the conflict should not overlook the fact that the infrastructure in conflict zones may already be in poor condition due to lack of maintenance and their repair after an attack may take longer in times of armed conflict. Especially in protracted conflicts, the death or absence of the personnel and the lack of necessary tools and parts add to the difficulties in repairing damaged water infrastructure.[128] For the purposes of the calculation of proportionality, the parties are also urged to take into consideration the expense and time required to repair the damage caused by the attack, and to keep

---

Proportionality Report, *supra* note 113, at 36–37; Gillard, *supra* note 110, para 107: 'The negotiating history of Additional Protocol I does not suggest that it was the intention of the drafters to exclude diseases.... Excluding disease could give rise to absurd results, for example, requiring expected injuries caused by the blast of nuclear weapons to be considered, but not those caused by the exposure to radiation from the same attack'.

125 According to Gillard, displacement does not in itself constitute incidental harm, but its likelihood should add to the weight given to the expected civilian harm (Gillard, *supra* note 110, para 74).

126 See ICRC Urban Services Report, *supra* note 6, at 14.

127 See, for example, Report of the Independent International Commission of Inquiry on the Syrian Arab Republic, *supra* note 124, para 45: 'On 31 July, intensified clashes damaged the electricity transmission station that facilitated power for pumping water to both eastern and western Aleppo city. Even though technicians were able to install a tributary power line on 4 August, the line sustained damage the next day. By 9 August and during a period of intense heat, approximately 1.7 million people throughout Aleppo city were left without access to running water'.

128 See ICRC Proportionality Report, *supra* note 113, at 45; Gillard, *supra* note 110, para 47: 'Another example would be an attack expected to damage a water purification facility in a country that is under sanctions and that, consequently, cannot acquire the necessary spare parts to repair the damage. The incidental harm expected to occur is caused by the attack even though it is amplified by the effect of the sanctions. While the imposition of sanctions is the conduct of a different actor, the harm ... is caused by the physical effects of the attack and must therefore be considered'.

in mind possible obstacles to carrying out repairs due to a lack of security and access.[129]

9. Notwithstanding the difficulties arising from the complex calculation of proportionality, it is accepted that the interpretation of this principle is a 'question of common sense and good faith for the military commanders', who should 'carefully weigh up the humanitarian and military interests at stake'.[130] The proportionality assessment should be carried out on the basis of information available to them at the time, after information from all sources regarding the potential targets and the effects of their targeting is gathered.[131]

2.10 *Principle 10: Precautions in Attack*

1. In the conduct of military operations, constant care must be taken to spare the civilian population, civilians and civilian objects, including water infrastructure and water-related infrastructure.
2. Prior to an attack against water infrastructure or water-related infrastructure, those who plan, decide upon and execute attacks must do everything feasible to verify that these are military objectives and that it is not prohibited to attack them.
3. Those who plan, decide upon and execute attacks, including against water infrastructure and water-related infrastructure, must take all feasible precautions with a view to avoiding, and in any event to minimizing, incidental loss of civilian life, injury to civilians and damage to civilian objects, including water infrastructure and water-related infrastructure.

2.10.1 Commentary

1. This principle reflects the principle of precautions under international humanitarian law, which is distinct from the precautionary principle under

129 See ICRC Proportionality Report, *supra* note 113, at 49–51; Gillard, *supra* note 110, paras 67–69. See also Separate Opinion of Hans Von Houtte in *Partial Award: Western Front, Aerial Bombardment and Related Claims 1, 3, 5, 9–13, 14, 21, 25 and 26* (*Eritrea v. Ethiopia*) (19 December 2005), 26 RIAA 291, at 346–349, para 11. It should also be noted that, by contrast, the possibility of repairing the damage done or of delivery of mitigating humanitarian assistance following an attack are considered too far-fetched to be considered in the proportionality assessment, in a way scaling down the expected harm.

130 ICRC Commentary, *supra* note 1, para 2208. See also *Prosecutor v. Stanislav Galić* (Judgment), Trial Chamber, IT-98-29-T (5 December 2003), para 58: 'In determining whether an attack was proportionate, it is necessary to examine whether a reasonably well-informed person in the circumstances of the actual perpetrator, making reasonable use of the information available to him or her, could have expected excessive civilian casualties to result from the attack' (footnotes omitted).

131 See also Principle 10 on precautions in attack.

international environmental law. The precautionary principle under the latter provides that '[w]here there are threats of serious or irreversible damage, lack of full scientific certainty shall not be used as a reason for postponing cost-effective measures to prevent environmental degradation'.[132] The precautionary principle under international environmental law is significant for the protection of the environment in general, but a detailed analysis of this principle falls outside the scope of the Geneva List.

2. The principle of precautions under international humanitarian law first of all requires that both the attacking and defending parties take constant care to spare the civilian population, civilians and civilian objects in the conduct of military operations.[133] This rule is part of customary international law applicable to international and non-international armed conflicts.[134] Military operations include, but are not limited to, attacks; consequently, the obligation to take constant care is applicable in a wider array of situations and not only during attacks.[135] Especially in their military operations, the parties to the conflict must take all feasible precautions to avoid all acts liable to destroy or damage water infrastructure indispensable to the survival of the civilian population, such as systems of water supply, purification and distribution.[136]

3. The principle of precautions encompasses several specific measures with respect to attacks, which are set forth both in treaty and customary international humanitarian law. These measures include, but are not limited to, the following: those who plan or decide upon an attack (a) must do everything feasible to verify that the objectives to be attacked are neither civilians nor civilian objects and are not subject to special protection but are military objectives and that it is not prohibited by international humanitarian law to attack them; (b) take all feasible precautions in the choice of means and methods of attack with a view to avoiding, and in any event to minimizing, incidental loss of civilian life, injury to civilians and damage to civilian objects; and (c) refrain

---

132 UN Conference on Environment and Development, *Rio Declaration on Environment and Development*, UN Doc A/CONF.151/26 (Vol. 1) (1992), Art. 15. This environmental law principle is notably reflected in the ICRC Customary IHL Study, *supra* note 35, Rule 44. See Principle 15 on protection of the environment.

133 Additional Protocol I, *supra* note 35, Art. 57(1).

134 ICRC Customary IHL Study, *supra* note 35, Rule 15.

135 ICRC Commentary, *supra* note 1, para 2191: 'The term "military operations" should be understood to mean any movements, manoeuvres and other activities whatsoever carried out by the armed forces with a view to combat'.

136 International Committee of the Red Cross, 'Protection of the civilian population in period of armed conflict', Resolution 2, 26th International Conference (7 December 1995), para F(b), https://www.icrc.org/en/doc/resources/documents/resolution/26-international-conference-resolution-2-1995.htm, accessed 12 June 2020.

from deciding to launch any attack which may be expected to cause incidental loss of civilian life, injury to civilians, damage to civilian objects, or a combination thereof, which would be excessive in relation to the concrete and direct military advantage anticipated.[137] Furthermore, an attack must be cancelled or suspended if it becomes apparent that the objective is not a military one or is subject to special protection or that the attack may be expected to cause incidental loss of civilian life, injury to civilians, damage to civilian objects, or a combination thereof, which would be excessive in relation to the concrete and direct military advantage anticipated.[138] Lastly, when a choice is possible between several military objectives for obtaining a similar military advantage, the objective to be selected must be the attack which may be expected to cause the least danger to civilian lives and to civilian objects.[139]

4. The specific precautions listed in the previous paragraph must be respected both in attacks against, and in attacks which may have effects on, water infrastructure and water-related infrastructure. Notwithstanding their importance, the body of the Principle only includes those precautions most pertinent to the protection of this infrastructure. Feasible precautions to be taken in cases of attacks against water infrastructure include, for example, the targeting of the pipe used by the military instead of the water reservoir itself, when the latter is used by both the military and civilian population.

5. Feasible precautions are those which are 'practicable or practically possible, taking into account all circumstances ruling at the time, including humanitarian and military considerations'.[140] Those who plan, decide upon

137 Additional Protocol I, *supra* note 35, Art. 57(2)(a)(i)–(iii). These rules are part of customary international law applicable to international and non-international armed conflicts (ICRC Customary IHL Study, *supra* note 35, Rules 16–18).

138 Additional Protocol I, *supra* note 35, Art. 57(2)(b). This rule is part of customary international law applicable to international and non-international armed conflicts (ICRC Customary IHL Study, *supra* note 35, Rule 19). See also Gillard, *supra* note 110, para 165: 'Belligerents must do what is feasible to monitor the battlefield constantly and to update the basis on which proportionality assessments are conducted to take changes into account'.

139 Additional Protocol I, *supra* note 35, Art. 57(3). This rule is part of customary international law applicable to international armed conflicts, and arguably also to non-international armed conflicts (ICRC Customary IHL Study, *supra* note 35, Rule 21).

140 Protocol on Prohibitions or Restrictions on the Use of Mines, Booby-Traps and other Devices as amended on 3 May 1996, annexed to the Convention on Prohibitions or Restrictions on the Use of Certain Conventional Weapons Which May Be Deemed to Be Excessively Injurious or to Have Indiscriminate Effects (3 May 1996), Art. 3(10) [Protocol II to the CCW]; Program on Humanitarian Policy and Conflict Research at Harvard University, *HPCR Manual on International Law Applicable to Air and Missile Warfare* (New York: Cambridge University Press, 2013), Rule 1(q) [HPCR Manual]; San

or execute an attack decide on the feasible precautions on the basis of their assessment of the information which is available to them at the relevant time.[141] Prior to all attacks, the parties to the conflict should undertake 'all feasible efforts' to gather reliable intelligence and use this intelligence in their assessments of attacks.[142] Information should be collected, for example, on the conditions and civilian uses of water infrastructure to be targeted, or which are expected to be affected by the attack; the dependency of the civilian population on this infrastructure and the nature of the area where the target is situated (for example, village, city, the natural environment surrounding the target).[143] Importantly, information on the possible incidental harm, including the reverberating effects, which may be caused to the civilian population and civilian objects, such as the environment, by the attacks, should be gathered.[144] Information on the presence of objects specially protected under international humanitarian law, including objects indispensable to the survival of the civilian population and works and installations containing dangerous forces should also be gathered.[145] The parties to the conflict are encouraged to set up

---

Remo Manual, *supra* note 118, para 46.3. This definition is reproduced in several military manuals (see, for example, US Manual (2015), *supra* note 89, para 5.2.3.2). See also Gillard, *supra* note 110, para 165: 'What is feasible in terms of verification once an attack has been launched varies in different types of attacks: those conducted by air or land forces, during combat engagement, or by forces with less sophisticated systems'.

141 ICRC Customary IHL Study, *supra* note 35, Commentary to Rule 15; Australia Manual (2006), *supra* note 75, para 5.11; HPCR Manual, *supra* note 140, Commentary to Rule 32(a), para 2. See also Gillard, *supra* note 110, para 168: 'The level of refinement of the analysis—that is, what information a belligerent can reasonably be expected to have, and therefore what incidental harm can be considered as reasonably foreseeable—will depend on the circumstances in which an attack is planned or conducted'.

142 HPCR Manual, *supra* note 140, Commentary to Rule 32(a), para 3.

143 Australia Manual (2006), *supra* note 75, para 5.54; France, *Fiche de Synthèse sur les Règles Applicables dans les Conflits Armés*, Note No. 432/DEF/EMA/OL.2/NP (1992), para 5.2 [France Summary Note].

144 In the context of the proportionality assessment, the Chatham Report sets forth that, *inter alia*, information on 'the effects of attacks on infrastructure that provides essential services to the civilian population', 'the impact of damage to such infrastructure on services, infrastructure and systems in the areas where the attacks will be carried out', 'the effect of the interruption of power supply on hospitals or water treatment facilities in the state where the attack will be conducted', 'the possible consequences of the attacks on elements of the natural environment' and 'the particular circumstances of the state where the attacks will be carried out, ... for example, if the state is subject to UN or other sanctions, blockades or other measures that could restrict its ability to repair damaged infrastructure' should be collected and taken into account (Gillard, *supra* note 110, para 169).

145 Australia Manual (2006), *supra* note 75, para 5.54; France Summary Note (1992), *supra* note 143, para 5.2.

a system to collect and analyse this information for use in their assessments of any attacks.[146]

2.11 *Principle 11: Precautions against the Effects of Attacks*

1. The parties to the conflict must take all feasible precautions to protect the civilian population and civilian objects, including water infrastructure and water-related infrastructure, under their control against the effects of attacks.
2. The parties to the conflict should avoid locating military objectives in the vicinity of water infrastructure and water-related infrastructure.
3. The parties to the conflict are encouraged to establish protected zones around water infrastructure and water-related infrastructure.

2.11.1 Commentary

1. Under international humanitarian law, defending parties also have precautionary obligations, also referred to as 'passive precautions'. First of all, they must take all feasible precautions to protect the civilian population and civilian objects under their control against the effects of attacks.[147] This rule is part of customary law applicable to international and non-international armed conflicts.[148] Additional Protocol I further and specifically requires that the parties to the conflict, to the maximum extent feasible, avoid locating military objectives, both permanent and mobile ones, within or near densely populated areas.[149] However, while this rule is applicable customarily to international armed conflicts, it is only arguably a part of customary international law applicable to non-international armed conflicts.[150]

2. The specific precautionary measures that can be taken with regard to water infrastructure include the identification and marking of existing

146 Gillard, *supra* note 110, para 168. See also International Criminal Tribunal for the Former Yugoslavia, *Final Report to the Prosecutor by the Committee Established to Review the NATO Bombing Campaign Against the Federal Republic of Yugoslavia* (13 June 2000), para 29: 'A military commander must set up an effective intelligence gathering system to collect and evaluate information concerning potential targets'.

147 Additional Protocol I, *supra* note 35, Art. 58(c). For more on the meaning of the term 'feasible', see Principle 9 on proportionality in attack.

148 ICRC Customary IHL Study, *supra* note 35, Rule 22. It should be noted that while Additional Protocol I, *supra* note 35, Article 58(c) refers to broader concept of military operations, the customary rule only covers attacks.

149 Additional Protocol I, *supra* note 35, Art. 58(b); ICRC Commentary, *supra* note 1, para 2251.

150 ICRC Customary IHL Study, *supra* note 35, Rule 23.

infrastructure.[151] States are also encouraged to include water infrastructure and related-infrastructure within the scope of critical infrastructure and take 'preparedness measures'.[152] The specific measure of avoiding locating military objectives in the vicinity of water infrastructure and water-related infrastructure follows the same rationale as the original rule explained in the first paragraph: avoiding large scale harm to the civilian population.

3. States that share transboundary watercourses also have an obligation to 'employ their best efforts to maintain and protect installations, facilities and other works related to an international watercourse'.[153] This rule entails an obligation to take all reasonable precautions to protect such works from foreseeable kinds of damage due to wilful human acts.[154] It should be noted that some of these measures can, and should, be already taken in peacetime, prior to armed conflicts.

4. In addition to the specific precautions against the effects of attacks, the parties to the conflict are also encouraged to establish protected zones around water infrastructure and water-related infrastructure. International humanitarian law provides for different types of protected zones, such as demilitarized zones and non-defended localities, which are aimed at the protection of the civilian population.[155] Notwithstanding the protective scopes of these zones as provided by law, the Geneva List encourages the parties to the conflict to set up protected zones around water infrastructure and water-related infrastructure as civilian objects vital for the civilian population. These zones can be set up unilaterally during peacetime and notified to the opposing parties in armed conflicts or through agreements between parties to a conflict. Preferably, the

---

151 Israel, 'Gaza Operation Investigations: Second Update', Ministry of Foreign Affairs of Israel (July 2010), para 151. See also Principle 13 on water infrastructure containing dangerous forces.

152 These measures have been proposed by the UN Security Council, in the context of terrorist acts against critical infrastructure. It is for each state to determine what constitutes its critical infrastructure (United Nations Security Council, '*Threats to international peace and security caused by terrorist acts*', 13 February 2017, UNSC Resolution 2341, UN Doc. S/RES/2341, Preamble and para 2).

153 UN Watercourses Convention, *supra* note 84, Art. 26(1).

154 ILC, '*Draft Articles on the Law of the Non-navigational Uses of International Watercourses and Commentaries Thereto and Resolution on Transboundary Confined Groundwater*', II:Part II, Yearbook of the International Law Commission (1994) 89–135, Commentary to Article 26, para 2 [ILC Draft Articles on Watercourses]. This Convention remains applicable during armed conflicts (Commentary to Article 29, para 3).

155 Additional Protocol I, *supra* note 35, Arts 59–60; ICRC Customary IHL Study, *supra* note 35, Rules 36–37 (applicable to both international and non-international armed conflicts).

notifications or the agreements should also provide for markings to identify the infrastructure.

2.12 *Principle 12: Starvation and Water Infrastructure Indispensable to the Survival of the Civilian Population*

1. The use of starvation of the civilian population as a method of warfare is prohibited.
2. The parties to the conflict must not attack, destroy, remove or render useless water infrastructure indispensable to the survival of the civilian population.

2.12.1 Commentary

1. The use of starvation of the civilian population as a method of warfare is prohibited.[156] This rule is part of customary international law applicable to international and non-international armed conflicts.[157] In its more restrictive meaning, starvation is 'killing by deprivation of water and food', but the deprivation of any essential commodity or thing necessary for survival is considered to be included in the definition of starvation.[158]

2. The prohibition of attacks against water infrastructure indispensable to the survival of the civilian population sets an absolute limit to the targeting of these objects.[159] This rule has also been included in the work of the ILA.[160] This infrastructure must not be made the object of reprisals.[161]

---

156 Additional Protocol I, *supra* note 35, Art. 54(1); Additional Protocol II, *supra* note 35, Art. 14. See also ICRC Commentary, *supra* note 1, para 2089: 'To use [starvation] as a method of warfare would be to provoke it deliberately, causing the population to suffer hunger, particularly by depriving it of its sources of food or of supplies'. The important issue of the effects of sieges, blockades and embargoes on the civilian population and their relation to the prohibition of starvation is beyond the scope of the Geneva List.

157 ICRC Customary IHL Study, *supra* note 35, Rule 53.

158 *Id.*, Commentary to Rule 54. The Commentary goes on to clarify that 'both Additional Protocols I and II consider food and medical supplies as essential to the survival of the civilian population, while Additional Protocol I also mentions clothing, bedding and means of shelter'. See also HPCR Manual, *supra* note 140, Commentary to Rule 97(a), para 2.

159 As opposed to the relativity of 'excessiveness' in the principle of proportionality. See Principle 9 on proportionality in attack.

160 Berlin Rules, *supra* note 32, Art. 51(2): 'In no event shall combatants attack, destroy, remove, or render useless waters and water installations indispensable for the health and survival of the civilian population if such actions may be expected to leave the civilian population with such inadequate water as to cause its death from lack of water or force its movement.'; Madrid Rules, *supra* note 32, Art. 2: 'Water supply installations which are indispensable for the minimum conditions of survival of the civilian population should not be cut off or destroyed'.

161 Additional Protocol I, *supra* note 35, Arts 52(1) and 54(4); ICRC Customary IHL Study, *supra* note 35, Rules 147–148.

3. Objects indispensable to the survival of the civilian population are all those which 'are of basic importance for the population from the point of view of providing the means of existence'.[162] Accordingly, they include both objects of sustenance as such and objects which contribute to their production.[163] Water infrastructure indispensable to the survival of the civilian population include, as expressly mentioned by Additional Protocol I, drinking water installations and supplies and irrigation works, but are not limited to them. It is accordingly prohibited to target any water infrastructure that contributes to the provision of objects indispensable to the survival of the population.

4. The prohibition covers not only attacks against water infrastructure, but also their destruction, removal and rendering useless.[164] Therefore, this prohibition extends to both 'attacks and other acts of destruction by one party against objects under the control of the adverse Party' and 'destruction by a Party of such items within its control'.[165] Indeed, the notions of 'removal' and 'rendering useless' imply control over the object and thus cover acts which are not necessarily against the adversary.[166] The prohibition thus covers (a) the harmful acts perpetrated by one party against water infrastructure indispensable to the survival of the population of the adverse party not under its control

162 ICRC Commentary, *supra* note 1, para 4803.

163 Official Records of the Diplomatic Conference on the Reaffirmation and Development of International Humanitarian Law Applicable in Armed Conflicts (Geneva, 1974–1977) (Federal Political Department, Bern 1978), Vol. XV, CDDH/III/264/Rev.1, at 349.

164 Additional Protocol I, *supra* note 35, Art. 54(2); Additional Protocol II, *supra* note 35, Art. 14. The ICRC Commentary explains that this wide range of acts are expressly listed in order to cover all possibilities and gives 'pollution, by chemical and other agents, of water reservoirs' as an example of a harmful act. See ICRC Commentary, *supra* note 1, para 2101.

165 M. Bothe, K. J. Partsch & W. A. Solf, *New Rules for Victims of Armed Conflicts: Commentary on the Two 1977 Protocols Additional to the Geneva Conventions 1949* (2nd edition, Leiden: Martinus Nijhoff Publishers, 2013), at 380–381, footnote 13. These two complementary obligations were initially provided in two different articles in the draft proposal of the ICRC. See 1977 Diplomatic Conference Records, *supra* note 163, Vol. XIV, CDDH/III/SR.37, at 395.

166 See, for example, von Lossow, 'Water as Weapon', *supra* note 72, at 2: 'After capturing the large dams at Falluja, Mosul, Samarra and Ramadi, IS not only interrupted local water supplies but also deprived distant Shiite areas in the lower reaches of the Euphrates and Tigris of water by damming and diverting it. In order to achieve this repeatedly stated goal of IS, water from the Euphrates was additionally diverted upstream in Syria. This meant, at the same time, that IS also struck at one of Iraq's most important agricultural centre [*sic*]'. Rendering useless can be realized by the mere act of 'turning off' the infrastructure. See, for example, Report of the Independent International Commission of Inquiry on the Syrian Arab Republic, *supra* note 124, para 47: 'On 23 September, the Suleiman al-Halabi pumping station located in the east was switched off, preventing water from reaching 1.5 million people in the western neighbourhoods of Aleppo city'.

and (b) the harmful acts against infrastructure situated in the territory under control of the party perpetrating the act.

5. A violation of this prohibition can also arise by omission. As explained by the ICRC Commentary, '[t]o deliberately decide not to take measures to supply the population with objects indispensable for its survival in a way would become a method of combat by default, and would be prohibited'.[167] An example of this would be ceasing to buy substances required for the purification of water and effectively depriving the civilian population of drinking water.

6. Water infrastructure can be rendered useless by means of targeting water-related infrastructure which are necessary to their functioning (for example, as their power source), such as electricity-generating facilities. This prohibition should thus be understood as also covering water-related infrastructure.

7. The acts of attack, destruction, removal or rendering useless should be carried out with the specific, but not the sole, purpose of denying these objects for their sustenance value to the civilian population or the adverse party of their sustenance.[168] The motive underlying the intent is irrelevant.[169] The element of purpose narrows down the scope of the special protection; a denial for other purposes or the mere incidental deprivation of sustenance would not fall within the scope of this rule.[170] However, the denial of the civilian population of their sustenance is an extreme impact. It is recommended that the intention of the party who carries out such harmful acts should be presumed to be denying their sustenance to the civilian population unless proven otherwise. In this regard, it is of note that many military manuals and national legislation

167 ICRC Commentary, *supra* note 1, para 4800. See also Principle 4 on use of water infrastructure and water-related infrastructure as a means of warfare.

168 Additional Protocol I, *supra* note 35, Art. 54(2); ICRC Customary IHL Study, *supra* note 35, Commentary to Rule 54. The reference to 'adverse party' separately from the 'civilian population' is explained by the ICRC Commentary as follows: '[T]he provision under consideration here means that it is prohibited to attack etc. objects indispensable to the survival of the civilian population wherever it is, or to deprive the enemy State of such objects indispensable to the civilian population' (ICRC Commentary, *supra* note 1, para 2107). The wording of the corresponding rule in Additional Protocol II is different; while it doesn't mention any specific purpose, it links this prohibition directly to that of starvation.

169 Tallinn Manual 2.0, *supra* note 89, at 532, Commentary to Rule 141, para 3.

170 *Id.*; ICRC Commentary, *supra* note 1, para 4807. See also 1977 Diplomatic Conference Records, *supra* note 163, Vol. XV, CDDH/III/264/Rev.1, at 349: '[B]ombarding an area to prevent the advance through it of an enemy is permissible, whether or not the area produces food, but the deliberate destruction of food producing areas in order to prevent the enemy from growing food on them is forbidden. Similarly, cutting down a field of crops in order to clear a field of fire or to prevent the enemy from using it for cover is permissible, but cutting it down to prevent the enemy from consuming the crops is forbidden'.

do not contain a requirement of purpose.[171] Lastly, acts which cause incidental deprivation of sustenance may in any case be in violation of other rules of international humanitarian law, especially the principles of distinction, proportionality and precautions.[172]

8. According to Additional Protocol I, the immunity of the objects indispensable to the survival of the civilian population against attacks is lifted if they are used (a) as sustenance solely for the members of a party's armed forces or (b) if not as sustenance, then in direct support of military action, provided that actions against these objects are not expected to leave the civilian population with such inadequate food or water as to cause its starvation or force its movement.[173] These exceptions are not provided for by Additional Protocol II.[174] The Geneva List also urges the parties to international armed conflicts to refrain from carrying out harmful acts under any circumstances, even if the conditions of the exceptions are met.[175]

9. According to Additional Protocol I, defending parties can derogate from this rule where required by imperative military necessity.[176] The derogation is allowed only in the party's national territory which is under its own control.[177] A party to the conflict, for example, may not flood its own territory under the control of the adverse party or a non-state armed group in order to take back territory that has already been lost.[178] Further, an Occupying Power may not derogate from the rule in the territories that it occupies, even if the destruction

171 See ICRC Customary IHL Study, *supra* note 35, Commentary to Rule 54.

172 See Principles 6–11 on principles on conduct of hostilities.

173 Additional Protocol I, *supra* note 35, Art. 54(3).

174 Additional Protocol II, *supra* note 35, Art. 14.

175 See also Tallinn Manual 2.0, *supra* note 89, at 533, Commentary to Rule 141, para 7.

176 Additional Protocol I, *supra* note 35, Art. 54(5). See also Berlin Rules, *supra* note 32, Art. 51(3): 'In recognition of the vital requirements of any party to a conflict in the defense of its national territory against invasion, a party to the conflict may derogate from the prohibitions [of destruction or diversion of waters and attacks against, destruction, removal and rendering useless of water installations indispensable for the health and survival of the civilian population] within such territories under its own control where required by imperative military necessity'.

177 According to the ICRC Commentary, '[t]he words "under its own control" refer to *de facto* control, i.e., the ability to exercise effective control' (ICRC Commentary, *supra* note 1, para 2118). See also 1977 Diplomatic Conference Records, *supra* note 163, Vol. XV, CDDH/407/Rev.1, p. 463: 'It should be noted that the term "control" in both paragraphs refers to areas of de facto control. In paragraph 1 it is the area under control of the Occupying Power, and in paragraph 2 it is the area of national territory remaining under the de facto control of the lawful sovereign. It goes without saying that the Occupying Power may not treat the occupied territory as if it were its national territory'.

178 ICRC Commentary, *supra* note 1, paras 2119, 2122.

of the object in question is rendered absolutely necessary by military operations.[179] This derogation is not provided for in Additional Protocol II.[180] The Geneva List also urges the parties to international armed conflicts to refrain from resorting to this derogation.

2.13 *Principle 13: Water Infrastructure Containing Dangerous Forces*

1. Water infrastructure containing dangerous forces, namely dams and dykes, even when these are military objectives, and other military objectives located at or in their vicinity, should not be made the object of attack, if such attack may cause the release of dangerous forces and consequent severe losses among the civilian population.
2. In any case, particular care must be taken if dams, dykes and other installations located at or in their vicinity are attacked, in order to avoid release of dangerous forces and consequent severe losses among the civilian population.
3. The parties to the conflict are encouraged to extend the protection provided for dams and dykes to all water infrastructure containing dangerous forces.

2.13.1 Commentary

1. Under Additional Protocols I and II, attacks against works and installations containing dangerous forces are prohibited, with very limited exceptions, which are dealt with below.[181] This rule is not identically reflected in customary international law. Indeed, according to the ICRC Customary International Humanitarian Law (IHL) Study, the parties to the conflict only have an obligation to take particular care if works and installations containing dangerous forces are attacked in order to avoid the release of dangerous forces and

179 *Id.*, para 2123. See also para 2120: 'As regards Occupying Powers, Article 53 of the Geneva Convention IV of 1949 prohibits the destruction of real or personal property, except where such destruction is rendered absolutely necessary by military operations. This is a general rule which is now supplemented by the provisions of Article 54 of the Protocol as regards objects indispensable to the survival of the civilian population'.

180 See Additional Protocol II, *supra* note 35, Art. 14. However, there have been examples of defensive acts in violation of this rule by the Islamic State in Syria. See, for example, von Lossow, 'Water as Weapon', *supra* note 72, at 3: 'By releasing the dammed water ..., IS prevented a rapid advance onto its own positions by follow-on units of the Iraqi army. In Diyala Governorate, too, the militia repeatedly flooded villages to foil Iraqi troop advances'.

181 Additional Protocol I, *supra* note 35, Art. 56; Additional Protocol II, *supra* note 35, Art. 15.

consequent severe losses among the civilian population. This customary rule is applicable to international and non-international armed conflicts.[182]

2. The prohibition of attacks against water infrastructure containing dangerous forces based on the treaty law sets an absolute limit to the targeting of and the incidental damage to these objects. Indeed, the standard set forth, severe losses among the civilian population caused by the release of dangerous forces, is not relative to the expected military advantage.[183] What is required is that the release of dangerous forces and the consequent severe losses among the civilian population be foreseeable.[184] The protection then is 'automatic, irrespective of the civilian, military or combined use' of the infrastructure.[185] This water infrastructure and other military objectives at or in their vicinity must not be made the object of reprisals.[186] This rule is reflected in the work of the ILA concerning water and armed conflicts.[187]

3. According to Additional Protocol I, this special protection ceases only if the protected objects are used 'in regular, significant and direct support of military operations and if such attack is the only feasible way to terminate such

---

182 ICRC Customary IHL Study, *supra* note 35, Rule 42. See also HPCR Manual, *supra* note 139, Rule 36: 'In order to avoid the release of dangerous forces and consequent severe losses among the civilian population, particular care must be taken if works and installations containing dangerous forces, namely dams, dykes and nuclear electrical generating stations (as well as installations located in their vicinity) are attacked'.

183 As opposed to the relativity of 'excessiveness' in the principle of proportionality. (See Principle 9 on proportionality in attack.) Severity of the losses among the civilian population is the sole consideration for this rule. According to the ICRC Commentary, the interpretation of the word 'severe' is 'a matter of common sense and it must be applied in good faith on the basis of objective elements'. The examples of objective elements given by the Commentary are the proximity of the inhabited areas, the density of population and the lie of the land (ICRC Commentary, *supra* note 1, paras 2154, 4821).

184 Bothe Commentary, *supra* note 165, at 395–396.

185 ICRC Commentary, *supra* note 1, para 4820; 1977 Diplomatic Conference Records, *supra* note 162, Vol. XIV, CDDH/III/SR.18, at 154. Some delegations also set forth the importance of the relation between of the protection of these works and installations and the protection of the environment. See, for example, *Id.*, at 155.

186 Additional Protocol I, *supra* note 35, Arts 52(1), 56(4); ICRC Customary IHL Study, *supra* note 35, Rules 147–148.

187 Berlin Rules, *supra* note 32, Art. 53; Madrid Rules, *supra* note 32, Art. 4. See also draft Article 13(2) of the UN Watercourses Convention which was later omitted: 'Hydraulic installations and other facilities, associated with an international watercourse system and capable of releasing dangerous forces or substances, shall not be attacked, destroyed or damaged during peacetime, or in time of armed conflict unless such installations or facilities are demonstrably being used as part of an adversary's offensive military positions or apparatus'. See Third Report of Schwebel, *supra* note 67, at 169.

support'.[188] Additionally, dams and dykes can only be targeted if they are used for other than their normal functions.[189] This exception is not provided by Additional Protocol II.[190] The Geneva List urges the parties to the conflict that also in international armed conflicts, they refrain from carrying out attacks under any circumstances, even if the conditions of the exception are met. It should also be noted that

> installations erected for the sole purpose of defending the protected works or installations from attack are permissible and shall not themselves be made the object of attack, provided that they are not used in hostilities except for defensive actions necessary to respond to attacks against the protected works or installations and that their armament is limited to weapons capable only of repelling hostile action against the protected works of installations.[191]

4. The works and installations protected by this rule are (a) dams and dykes, even where these are military objectives, and (b) other military objectives located at or in the vicinity of these, if attacks against them may cause the release of dangerous forces and consequent severe losses among the civilian population.[192] Regarding the first category, admittedly, such water infrastructure is not the only type of infrastructure which may cause severe losses among the civilian population due to the release of dangerous forces. Consequently, the Geneva List urges the parties to the conflict to follow this rule also when other water infrastructure containing dangerous forces, such as wastewater treatment plants, are concerned.[193] It should also be noted that during the

---

188 Additional Protocol I, *supra* note 35, Art. 56(2).

189 *Id.*, Art. 56(2)(a). According to the ICRC Commentary 'the expression "other than its normal function" means that the dam or dyke is used for a purpose other than containing an actual or potential mass of water, which is the normal function of such a structure' (ICRC Commentary, *supra* note 1, para 2161). Regarding the usage of water infrastructure protected by this Article, i.e. dams and dykes, for other than their normal function and in regular, significant and direct support of the military operations, the ICRC Commentary gives the examples of a dyke which is a part of a fortifications system and a dam across the top of which there is an essential route for the movement of armed forces (para 2162).

190 Additional Protocol II, *supra* note 35, Art. 15.

191 Additional Protocol I, *supra* note 35, Art. 56(5).

192 *Id.*, Art. 56(1); Additional Protocol II, *supra* note 35, Art. 15. The prohibition of attacks against military objectives in the vicinity of dams and dykes are only set forth in Additional Protocol I.

193 See also ICRC Customary IHL Study, *supra* note 35, Commentary to Rule 42, which recommends that this rule also be applied to other works and installations containing dangerous forces: '[T]he considerations explained above should equally apply to other

Diplomatic Conference preceding the adoption of the Additional Protocols, a number of states have, albeit unsuccessfully, advocated for an illustrative, not exhaustive, list of works and installations containing dangerous forces.[194] Regarding the second category, it should be noted that the military objectives located at or in the vicinity can also consist of water-related infrastructure. It is further recommended by the Geneva List that, irrespective of the geographical proximity of a given water infrastructure and the water-related infrastructure it depends on, attacks against the latter be prohibited under this rule if such attack may cause the release of dangerous forces and consequent severe losses among the civilian population.

5. For the purposes of the recommendation to extend the protection to other water infrastructure containing dangerous forces, the term 'dangerous forces' means all forces which are perilous due to their volume or quality and if released, would cause severe losses among the civilian population in the short- or long-term.[195] For example, while dams and dykes pose a danger because of the volume of water they retain, wastewater treatment plants which contain contaminated water pose a danger due to the nature of the water they retain and may lead to the poisoning of the civilians or the degradation of the environment in the case of the release of this water.

6. The parties to the conflict are urged to conclude further agreements regarding the protection of objects containing dangerous forces.[196] These agreements can also be concluded in peacetime, prior to armed conflicts. Through these agreements, the parties can (a) provide additional protection to dams and dykes and (b) extend the protection provided to dams and dykes to other water infrastructure containing dangerous forces.[197]

---

installations, such as chemical plants and petroleum refineries. The fact that attacks on such installations may cause severe damage to the civilian population and the natural environment implies that the decision to attack such installations, in case they become military objectives, requires that all necessary precautions be taken when attacking them'.

194 See, for example, the proposals of Romania (CCCD/III/10); Belgium and Netherlands (CDDH /III/59) and Egypt together with 13 other countries (CDDH/III/76 and Add.1), in 1977 Diplomatic Conference Records, *supra* note 163, Vol. III, at 222–224. However, an agreement could only be reached on a list of limited objects. See also ICRC Commentary, *supra* note 1, paras 2146–2150.

195 It is of note that draft Article 13(2) of the UN Watercourses Convention, which was later omitted, referred both to dangerous forces and substances while reproducing this rule of international humanitarian law. See Third Report of Schwebel, *supra* note 67, at 169.

196 Additional Protocol I, *supra* note 35, Art. 56(6).

197 ICRC Commentary, *supra* note 1, para 2177. One of the suggested further measures of protection by the ICRC Commentary is the neutralization of the dams and dykes and the surrounding areas under the supervision of the Protecting Powers or other organizations. See also Principle 11 on the precautions against the effects of attacks.

FIGURE 1 International special sign for works and installations containing dangerous forces

7. The parties to the conflict are encouraged to mark dams, dykes and other water infrastructure containing dangerous forces with the special sign provided by Article 17 of Annex I to Additional Protocol I.[198] While this marking is not obligatory, its absence does not revoke the protection added to dams and dykes and thus does not relieve the attacking parties from their obligations.[199] In light of the technological developments, this infrastructure can also be identified with agreed-upon electronic markings, in addition to the physical markings with the special sign (Figure 1).[200]

8. The parties to conflict are encouraged to communicate a list of such infrastructure with their geographical location to the adversary through an intermediary to ensure better protection of the civilian population.[201] Also, states which share transboundary watercourses should continue to cooperate even in cases where there are serious obstacles to direct contact between them, including armed conflicts. This cooperation should include exchange of data and information, notification, communication, consultations and negotiations, through any indirect procedure accepted by them, unless the data or information is vital to their national defence or security.[202]

---

198 Additional Protocol I, *supra* note 35, Art. 56(7). For further information on how the special sign should be used, see Article 17 of Annex I to Protocol Additional I to the Geneva Conventions of 1949: Regulations Concerning Identification, as amended on 30 November 1993.

199 ICRC Commentary, *supra* note 1, para 2182.

200 See Tallinn Manual 2.0, *supra* note 90, at 531, Commentary to Rule 140, para 8.

201 ICRC Commentary, *supra* note 1, para 2182.

202 UN Watercourses Convention, *supra* note 84, Arts 30–31. In any case '[t]he State [withholding data or information vital to its national defence or security] shall cooperate in good faith with the other watercourse States with a view to providing as much information as possible under the circumstances' (Article 31). For examples of continued indirect communication between watercourse states during armed conflicts, see Principle 20 on joint mechanisms and commissions.

2.14 *Principle 14: Acts or Threats of Violence the Primary Purpose of Which is to Spread Terror among the Civilian Population*

Acts or threats of violence the primary purpose of which is to spread terror among the civilian population, including but not limited to the release of dangerous forces from dams and dykes, and the poisoning or retention of water, are prohibited.

2.14.1 Commentary

1. Acts or threats of violence the primary purpose of which is to spread terror among the civilian population are prohibited under international humanitarian law.[203] This rule is part of customary law applicable to international and non-international armed conflicts.[204]

2. Water infrastructure can be the instrument of acts or threats of violence aiming at spreading terror among the civilian population in many ways. First of all, in the case of large water infrastructure such as dams or dykes, parties can threaten to either release the dangerous forces contained therein if they have control over such infrastructure, or to attack such infrastructure, if it is under the control of the opposing party. The severe consequences of acting on such threats include the destruction of houses, arable lands and displacement of large numbers of civilians.[205] The parties to the conflict may also threaten to poison or cut the water supply with a view to terrorizing the civilian population. Accordingly, in addition to the prohibition of using water infrastructure as a means of warfare, using them as a tool to spread terror is also prohibited.[206]

2.15 *Principle 15: Protection of the Environment*

Water infrastructure and water-related infrastructure should not be made the object of attack, even when these are military objectives, if

---

203 Additional Protocol I, *supra* note 35, Art. 51(2); Additional Protocol II, *supra* note 35, Art. 13(2). See also ICRC Commentary, *supra* note 1, para 1940: 'In the second sentence the Conference wished to indicate that the prohibition covers acts intended to spread terror; there is no doubt that acts of violence related to a state of war almost always give rise to some degree of terror among the population and sometimes also among the armed forces.... This provision is intended to prohibit acts of violence the primary purpose of which is to spread terror among the civilian population without offering substantial military advantage. It is interesting to note that threats of such acts are also prohibited'.

204 ICRC Customary IHL Study, *supra* note 35, Rule 2.

205 See also Principle 13 on water infrastructure containing dangerous forces.

206 See Principle 4 on use of water infrastructure and water-related infrastructure as a means of warfare.

such attack is intended, or may be expected, to cause significant damage to the environment.

2.15.1 Commentary

1. Under international humanitarian law, the natural environment is protected by the general principles on the conduct of hostilities, both in international and non-international armed conflicts.[207] The specific protection of the natural environment is set forth in Articles 35(3) and 55 of Additional Protocol I. These articles prohibit the use of methods or means of warfare that are intended or may be expected to cause widespread, long-term and severe damage to the natural environment.[208] This prohibition is part of customary international law applicable to international armed conflicts, and arguably also to non-international armed conflicts.[209] More generally, Additional Protocol I requires that care be taken to protect the natural environment against widespread, long-term and severe damage.[210] This duty of due regard is also part of customary international law applicable to international armed conflicts, and arguably also to non-international armed conflicts.[211]

2. In setting forth the above protection regime, international humanitarian law invariably refers to the 'natural environment'. This concept is defined as

---

207 ICRC Customary IHL Study, *supra* note 35, Rule 43: 'The general principles on the conduct of hostilities apply to the natural environment: A. No part of the natural environment may be attacked, unless it is a military objective. B. Destruction of any part of the natural environment is prohibited, unless required by imperative military necessity. C. Launching an attack against a military objective which may be expected to cause incidental damage to the environment which would be excessive in relation to the concrete and direct military advantage anticipated is prohibited'. See also ILC, *Protection of the Environment in Relation to Armed Conflict, supra* note 20, Draft Principle 14; ICRC, '*Guidelines for Military Manuals and Instructions on the Protection of the Environment in Times of Armed Conflict*', 311, International Review of the Red Cross (30 April 1994), para 4.

208 Article 35(3) addresses the protection of the natural environment as such and Article 55 in relation to the protection of the civilian population.

209 ICRC Customary IHL Study, *supra* note 35, Rule 45. This rule also prohibits the use of destruction of the natural environment as a weapon.

210 Additional Protocol I, *supra* note 35, Art. 55. See also ILC, *Protection of the Environment in Relation to Armed Conflict, supra* note 20, Draft Principle 13(2).

211 ICRC Customary IHL Study, *supra* note 35, Rule 44: 'Methods and means of warfare must be employed with due regard to the protection and preservation of the natural environment. In the conduct of military operations, all feasible precautions must be taken to avoid, and in any event to minimize, incidental damage to the environment. Lack of scientific certainty as to the effects on the environment of certain military operations does not absolve a party to the conflict from taking such precautions'. The last part of this rule is based on the precautionary principle under international environmental law (see also the commentary to Principle 10 on precautions in attack).

covering 'the biological environment in which a population is living' in the widest sense, including 'forests and other vegetation …, as well as fauna, flora, and other biological or climatic elements'.[212] In line with the ongoing work of the ILC on the protection of the environment in relation to armed conflicts, the Geneva List opts for the term 'environment'. At the time of writing, the last report of the Special Rapporteur has proposed not to include a definition of the term 'environment' given that there is no agreed definition in international law.[213] Likewise, the Geneva List will also abstain from defining the notion.

3. The protection of the natural environment under international humanitarian law is only against widespread, long-term *and* severe damage. In other words, the prohibition of using certain means and methods of warfare requires a cumulative threshold. Likewise, the ILA's Berlin Rules prohibit the destruction or diversion of waters and the destruction of water installations when such an act 'would cause widespread, long-term, and severe ecological damage prejudicial to the health or survival of the population or if such acts would fundamentally impair the ecological integrity of waters'.[214] On the other hand, the Convention on the Prohibition of Military or any Other Hostile Use of Environmental Modification Techniques prohibits modification techniques the effects of which are widespread, long-term *or* severe.[215] Lastly, the ILA's Madrid Rules, which were drafted before the adoption of the Additional Protocols, systematically refer to 'substantial damage' as a threshold for the protection of the 'ecological balance' during armed conflicts.[216]

4. In the context of the regulation of transboundary harm, the most extensively used threshold is that of 'significant harm'. For example, the UN Watercourses Convention stipulates that 'in utilizing an international

212 ICRC Commentary, *supra* note 1, para 2126.

213 ILC, *Second Report on Protection of the Environment in Relation to Armed Conflicts by Marja Lehto, Special Rapporteur*, Doc A/CN.4/728 (27 March 2019), paras 186–193. The Commission has nevertheless defined the term 'environment' in its previous work. See ILC, '*Draft Principles on the Allocation of Loss in the Case of Transboundary Harm Arising Out of Hazardous Activities*', II:Part II, Yearbook of the International Law Commission (2006) 59–90, Principle 2(b): '"[E]nvironment" includes natural resources, both abiotic and biotic, such as air, water, soil, fauna and flora and the interaction between the same factors, and the characteristic aspects of the landscape'.

214 Berlin Rules, *supra* note 32, Art. 52.

215 Convention on the Prohibition of Military or Any Other Hostile Use of Environmental Modification Techniques (10 December 1976), Art. 1(1): 'Each State Party to this Convention undertakes not to engage in military or any other hostile use of environmental modification techniques having widespread, long-lasting or severe effects as the means of destruction, damage or injury to any other State Party'.

216 Madrid Rules, *supra* note 32, Arts 3–5.

watercourse in their territories', watercourse states 'take all appropriate measures to prevent causing of significant harm to other watercourse States'.[217] The 'significant' threshold has also been confirmed by the ICJ in the context of protection of the environment. According to the Court, the obligation of a state to 'use all the means at its disposal in order to avoid activities which take place in its territory, or in any area under its jurisdiction, causing significant damage to the environment of another State' is 'part of the corpus of international law relating to the environment'.[218] According to the ILC, the meaning of 'significant' has to be determined on a case-by-case basis, based on the specific facts. The Commission continues:

> It is to be understood that 'significant' is something more than 'detectable' but need not be at the level of 'serious' or 'substantial'. The harm must lead to a real detrimental effect on matters such as, for example, human health, industry, property, environment or agriculture in other States. Such detrimental effects must be susceptible of being measured by factual and objective standards.[219]

217 UN Watercourses Convention, *supra* note 84, Art. 7. See also Article 21(2): 'Watercourse States shall, individually and, where appropriate, jointly, prevent, reduce and control the pollution of an international watercourse that may cause significant harm to other watercourse States or to their environment, including harm to human health or safety, to the use of the waters for any beneficial purpose or to the living resources of the watercourse'. See also Convention on Environmental Impact Assessment in a Transboundary Context (25 February 1991), Art. 2(1): 'The Parties shall, either individually or jointly, take all appropriate and effective measures to prevent, reduce and control significant adverse transboundary environmental impact from proposed activities.'; UNECE Convention, *supra* note 84, Article 2(1): 'The Parties shall take all appropriate measures to prevent, control and reduce any transboundary impact'. According to Article 1(2) of the UNECE Convention, 'transboundary impact' means 'any significant adverse effect on the environment resulting from a change in the conditions of transboundary waters caused by a human activity, the physical origin of which is situated wholly or in part within an area under the jurisdiction of a Party, within an area under the jurisdiction of another Party'.

218 ICJ, Case concerning Pulp Mills on the River Uruguay (Argentina v. Uruguay), Judgment, 20 April 2010, para 101; Nuclear Weapons Advisory Opinion, *supra* note 72, para 29. See also ICJ, Case concerning the Gabčíkovo-Nagymaros Project (Hungary v. Slovakia), Judgment, 25 September 1997, para 140: '[I]n the field of environmental protection, vigilance and prevention are required on account of the often irreversible character of damage to the environment and of the limitations inherent in the very mechanism of reparation of this type of damage'.

219 ILC, '*Draft Articles on Prevention of Transboundary Harm from Hazardous Activities*', II: Part II, Yearbook of the International Law Commission (2001) 148–170, Commentary to Article 2, para 4. See also UNECE Convention, *supra* note 84, Article 1(2): '[Significant adverse] effects on the environment include effects on human health and safety, flora,

In the light of the developments in international water law and international environmental law, the Geneva List opts for putting the threshold at 'significant damage'. Consequently, this Principle departs from the international humanitarian law rule, which is binding on the parties to the conflicts and constitutes a recommendation.

5. Attacks against water infrastructure, especially certain types such as wastewater treatment plants, can cause significant damage to the environment. Water treatment plants and pumping stations may have reserves of toxic industrial chemicals, such as substances for the treatment of water or fuel for back-up generators, which can potentially have significant adverse effects on the environment if released. The damage to the environment can include the contamination of surface and groundwater resources, and degradation of flora, fauna and soil. These constitute not only significant damage to the environment, but also grave risks for the health and livelihoods of the civilian population.

6. In cases where an attack is not intended to or may be expected to cause significant damage to the natural environment, the said attack is governed by the principles of proportionality and precautions. Even when they do not meet the widespread, long-term and severe, or significant thresholds, attacks against water infrastructure and water-related infrastructure can have adverse effects on the environment. The foreseeable reverberating effects of these attacks on the environment should be taken into account in the calculation of proportionality.[220] States should carry out environmental impact assessments prior to engaging in any attack against water infrastructure and water-related infrastructure, especially when these contain, qualitatively or quantitatively, substances which may have adverse effects on the environment.

2.16 *Principle 16: Forced Displacement*

The control over the delivery of water, and deprivation thereof, must not be used to force the displacement of civilians.

---

fauna, soil, air, water, climate, landscape and historical monuments or other physical structures or the interaction among these factors; they also include effects on the cultural heritage or socio-economic conditions resulting from alterations to those factors'.

220 Nuclear Weapons Advisory Opinion, *supra* note 72, para 30: 'States must take environmental considerations into account when assessing what is necessary and proportionate in the pursuit of legitimate military objectives. Respect for the environment is one of the elements that go to assessing whether an action is in conformity with the principles of necessity and proportionality'. For more on reverberating effects, see Principle 9 on proportionality in attack.

2.16.1 Commentary

1. Forced displacement is prohibited under international humanitarian law. In international armed conflicts, the Fourth Geneva Convention prohibits individual or mass forcible transfers and deportations of protected persons from occupied territories.[221] In non-international armed conflicts, Additional Protocol II stipulates that the displacement of the civilian population must not be ordered for reasons related to the conflict unless the security of the civilians involved or imperative military reasons so demand. Additionally, it states that civilians must not be compelled to leave their own territory for reasons related to the conflict.[222] These rules are partly reflected in customary international law applicable to international and non-international armed conflicts respectively.[223]

2. The Guiding Principles on Internal Displacement, a non-binding yet widely-accepted document, sets forth that '[e]very human being shall have the right to be protected against being arbitrarily displaced from his or her home or place of habitual residence'.[224] The UN Human Rights Committee has also interpreted freedom of movement as including a protection against all forms of forced internal displacement.[225]

3. Targeting of water infrastructure can cause both immediate displacement and displacement in the mid- to long-terms. An example of the former is damaging or destruction of a dam, directly causing the inundation of downstream

221 Geneva Convention IV, *supra* note 35, Art. 49.

222 Additional Protocol II, *supra* note 35, Art. 17.

223 ICRC Customary IHL Study, *supra* note 35, Rule 129: 'A. Parties to an international armed conflict may not deport or forcibly transfer the civilian population of an occupied territory, in whole or in part, unless the security of the civilians involved or imperative military reasons so demand. B. Parties to a non-international armed conflict may not order the displacement of the civilian population, in whole or in part, for reasons related to the conflict, unless the security of the civilians involved or imperative military reasons so demand'.

224 United Nations Economic and Social Council, *Guiding Principles on Internal Displacement*, UN Doc E/CN.4/1998/53/Add.2 (11 February 1998), Principle 6(1).

225 UN Human Rights Committee, *General Comment No. 27: Freedom of Movement (Article 12)*', UN Doc CCPR/C/21/Rev.1/Add.9 (1 November 1999), para 7. See also UN Committee on Economic, Social and Cultural Rights, 'General Comment No. 7: The right to adequate housing (Art. 11(1) of the Covenant): Forced evictions' (1997), para 5: 'Although the practice of forced evictions might appear to occur primarily in heavily populated urban areas, it also takes place in connection with forced population transfers, internal displacement, forced relocations in the context of armed conflict, mass exoduses and refugee movements. In all of these contexts, the right to adequate housing and not to be subjected to forced eviction may be violated through a wide range of acts or omissions attributable to States parties'.

lands, which can compel the local population to move. An example of the latter is the case where an irrigation infrastructure is destroyed or otherwise rendered useless, causing the loss of the livelihood of the community, which can also force them to move in the future, as opposed to directly after the attack.[226]

4. This Principle deals with situations in which civilians are forcibly displaced by parties who have control over the water infrastructure, without resorting to attacks against water infrastructure. Indeed, parties who have control over water infrastructure can force the displacement of civilians through depriving them of water for drinking, sanitation and other domestic uses and irrigation.[227] Likewise, if a party has control over larger water infrastructure, such as dams, they may force civilians to move by means of threats or acts of flooding.[228]

5. A related issue which is not dealt with in the text of the Principle but nevertheless should be mentioned here is the return of displaced persons. According to the ICRC Customary IHL Study, '[d]isplaced persons have a right to voluntary return in safety to their homes or places of habitual residence as soon as the reasons for their displacement cease to exist'.[229] This customary rule is applicable to international and non-international armed conflicts. All those voluntarily returning should be provided with the means to do so in safety and with dignity.[230] In this regard, returnees' access to water should be ensured through the reconstruction, rehabilitation and repair of water infrastructure as needed.[231]

2.17 *Principle 17: Humanitarian Access and Assistance*

1. Humanitarian relief personnel, including those involved in water-related activities, and their equipment must be respected and protected.

---

226 See also Principle 9 on proportionality in attack.

227 Here it should be remembered that the parties to the conflict should also ensure the delivery of water to the civilian population equally and without discrimination. See also Principle 3 on the human rights to water and sanitation.

228 These acts or threats can be, and have been, carried out with a view to gaining control over more land, resulting in the displacement of civilians over whom the acting or threatening party does not have control. See also Principles 4 and 14 on use of water infrastructure as a means of warfare and acts or threats of violence the primary purpose of which is to spread terror among the civilian population respectively.

229 ICRC Customary IHL Study, *supra* note 35, Rule 132.

230 Guiding Principles on Internal Displacement, *supra* note 224, Principle 28(1).

231 See Principle 21 on reconstruction, rehabilitation and repair of water infrastructure and water-related infrastructure. See also Report of the Special Rapporteur on the Human Rights to Safe Drinking Water and Sanitation, *supra* note 26, paras 51–52.

2. The parties to the conflict must allow and facilitate rapid and unimpeded passage of humanitarian relief personnel, including those involved in water-related activities, and their equipment for the operation, maintenance, assessment, repair and rehabilitation of water infrastructure and water-related infrastructure, especially those which provide water indispensable to the survival of the civilian population.
3. Civil defence organizations, including those involved in the repair and rehabilitation of water infrastructure and water-related infrastructure, and their personnel must be respected and protected.
4. The parties to the conflict are encouraged to negotiate water ceasefire agreements in order to allow the safe passage of humanitarian relief personnel, including those involved in water-related activities.
5. The parties to the conflict are encouraged to collaborate for the operation, maintenance, assessment, repair and rehabilitation of water infrastructure and water-related infrastructure.

2.17.1 Commentary

1. Humanitarian relief personnel, including personnel involved in water-related activities and in the repair and rehabilitation of water infrastructure and water-related infrastructure (hereinafter water-related personnel), must be respected and protected. Such personnel include, but are not limited to, engineers, operators, technicians and repair crews. Likewise, objects used for humanitarian relief operations, including the equipment necessary to carry out the repair and rehabilitation of the infrastructure, must also be respected and protected.[232] Such equipment include, for example, spare parts for the infrastructure and the chemical substances necessary for the purification of water. These rules are part of customary international law applicable to international and non-international armed conflicts.[233]

2. The parties to the conflict have obligations to (a) allow and facilitate rapid and unimpeded passage of humanitarian relief for civilians in need, subject to their right of control, and (b) to ensure the freedom of movement of humanitarian relief personnel, unless imperative military necessity requires

232 Additional Protocol I, *supra* note 35, Arts 70(4), 71(2).

233 ICRC Customary IHL Study, *supra* note 35, Rules 31–32. See also Commentary to Rule 31: 'While the Additional Protocols provide that the protection of humanitarian relief personnel applies only to "authorized" humanitarian personnel as such, the overwhelming majority of practice does not specify this condition. The notion of authorization refers to the consent received from the party to the conflict concerned to work in areas under its control. Authorization may not be withheld for arbitrary reasons to deny access to humanitarian relief personnel' (footnotes omitted).

otherwise.[234] These rules are part of customary international law applicable to international and non-international armed conflicts.[235] While relief operations are subject to the consent of the concerned party to the conflict, this consent cannot be withheld arbitrarily.[236] Water-related personnel and their equipment should be allowed rapid and unimpeded passage and access to water infrastructure requiring repair and rehabilitation.[237]

3. Water is indispensable for the survival of the civilian population; in cases where the civilian population's access to water cannot be ensured by the concerned party to the conflict, humanitarian relief operations must be allowed to ensure this access. Denying access of humanitarian aid, including deliberately impeding it, or restricting the freedom of movement of the humanitarian relief personnel may under certain circumstances constitute violations of the prohibition of starvation.[238] This would be the case when there is a direct link between the starvation of the civilian population and the damaging or destruction of water infrastructure, such as drinking water installations and supplies and irrigation works. Where there is a shortage of drinking water or disruption of food production resulting in starvation due to the damaging or destruction of water infrastructure, water-related personnel must be given access to the damaged water infrastructure to ensure its operation. Likewise, the equipment necessary for the repair and rehabilitation of the water infrastructure must be given rapid and unimpeded passage.

4. Additional Protocol I provides for the protection regime of civil defence organizations.[239] While there is no such regime foreseen in Additional Protocol II, it is submitted that these organizations should be respected and protected in non-international armed conflicts as in international armed conflicts, in line with the general protection of the civilian population against the

---

234 Additional Protocol I, *supra* note 35, Arts 70–71.

235 ICRC Customary IHL Study, *supra* note 35, Rules 55–56.

236 *Id.*, Commentary to Rule 55.

237 This need or repair and rehabilitation can be due to both the effects of hostilities or lack of maintenance. See also United Nations General Assembly, '*The Situation in Bosnia and Herzegovina*', 20 December 1993, UNGA Resolution 48/88, UN Doc. A/RES/48/88, para 12: 'Demands that all concerned facilitate the unhindered flow of humanitarian assistance, including the provision of water, electricity, fuel and communication, in particular to the "safe areas" in Bosnia and Herzegovina, and in this context urges the Security Council to implement fully its resolution 770 (1992) to ensure the free flow of humanitarian assistance, particularly, to the "safe areas"'.

238 ICRC Customary IHL Study, *supra* note 35, Commentary to Rule 53. See also ICRC Commentary, *supra* note 1, para 2808.

239 Additional Protocol I, *supra* note 35, Arts 61–67.

dangers arising from military operations.[240] The enumerated tasks of civil defence organizations include the provision of emergency accommodation and supplies, emergency repair of indispensable public utilities and assistance in the preservation of objects essential for survival.[241] These activities naturally cover ensuring the civilian population's access to water and the repair and rehabilitation of water infrastructure as indispensable public utilities. The performance of civil defence tasks must be allowed at all times, and can only be denied in case of imperative military necessity.[242] Furthermore, the protection of civilian defence organizations, their personnel and equipment only ceases if they commit or are used to commit, outside their proper tasks, acts harmful to the enemy.[243]

5. In times of armed conflict, the rehabilitation and reconstruction of water infrastructure may be unduly delayed, despite their vital character.[244] The parties to the conflict are thus encouraged to undertake negotiations towards humanitarian ceasefires.[245] The ceasefire agreements should expressly include ensuring the safe and unimpeded access to water infrastructure of the water-related personnel and the equipment necessary for the repair and rehabilitation of water infrastructure to the damaged infrastructure.[246] This is particularly important since the negotiations between the parties to the conflict and humanitarian organizations on safe access in most cases are lengthy and burdensome and are required every time a relief activity is undertaken. An

240 ICRC, '*Civil Defence in International Humanitarian Law*', Factsheet (2001).

241 Additional Protocol I, *supra* note 35, Art. 61(a)(x), (xii), (xiv).

242 *Id.*, Art. 62(1).

243 *Id.*, Art. 65(1).

244 See United Nations Secretary-General, 'Joint Statement by the Secretary-General and US Secretary of State John Kerry on Humanitarian Ceasefire Announcement' (31 July 2014), https://www.un.org/sg/en/content/sg/statement/2014-07-31/joint-statement-secretary-general-and-us-secretary-state-john-kerry, accessed 12 June 2020: 'This ceasefire is critical to giving innocent civilians a much-needed reprieve from violence.... Overdue repairs on essential water and energy infrastructure could also continue during this period'.

245 For the purposes of the Geneva List, a ceasefire agreement is an agreement between the parties to the conflict to temporarily halt hostilities for humanitarian reasons.

246 A number of ceasefires were successfully concluded in Ukraine to allow for the repair of damaged water infrastructure. See, for example, Organization for Security and Co-operation in Europe, Special Monitoring Mission to Ukraine, *Access to Water in Conflict-affected Areas of Donetsk and Luhansk Regions* (Vienna: OSCE, 2015), pp. 11–13. See also Humanitarian Ceasefire Agreement on the Conflict in Darfur (8 April 2004), Art. 1: 'The ceasefire will be effective on land, and air, to allow ... a fast and unrestricted humanitarian access to the needy populations of Darfur'.

agreement between the parties to the conflict would facilitate the work of these organizations and consequently alleviate the civilian population's suffering.[247]

6. The UN Security Council has already called for temporary ceasefires on humanitarian grounds.[248] The Geneva List suggests that the Council also encourages 'water supply ceasefires' and expressly refers to water infrastructure and water-related infrastructure in its resolutions.[249]

7. As a last remark, situations where the party who has control over a certain water infrastructure or water-related infrastructure change should be mentioned. During armed conflicts, the party who has built and has been operating the infrastructure may lose its control over the infrastructure to the opposing party. Particularly in these cases, in order to facilitate the operation, maintenance, assessment, repair and rehabilitation of water infrastructure and water-related infrastructure, the Geneva List encourages the parties to the conflict to collaborate. This collaboration can be by means of sharing the information and expertise that may not only be useful but in some cases indispensable for the general functioning of the infrastructure. Therefore it may be crucial for the continuation of basic services for the benefit of the civilian population.[250]

---

247 See, for example, ICRC, *Bled Dry: How War in the Middle East Is Bringing the Region's Water Supplies to breaking Point* (Geneva: ICRC, 2015), at 30: '"I spend most of my time on diplomacy and negotiation," says David Kaelin, ICRC water and habitat coordinator in Syria. One case-in-point came after a main water transmission pipeline, which supplies water to Hama, a city of almost 1.3 million people, was damaged in the fighting. The ICRC needed to go in with the water board to do an assessment, but it needed a guarantee of safety. "It took almost 3 weeks to do the actual negotiation to get access," recalls Talhami. "Whereas it took less than 1 week to actually do the repairs. This is why we often say that to do an emergency response it's less about the technical side and the ability of the contractors to perform the work, and more about the politics and negotiations that are necessary to ensure that you have safe access"'.

248 See, for example, United Nations Security Council, '*The situation in the Middle East*', 24 February 2018, UNSC Resolution 2401, UN Doc. S/RES/2401, para 1: 'Demands that all parties cease hostilities without delay, and engage immediately to ensure full and comprehensive implementation of this demand by all parties, for a durable humanitarian pause for at least 30 consecutive days throughout Syria, to enable the safe, unimpeded and sustained delivery of humanitarian aid and services and medical evacuations of the critically sick and wounded, in accordance with applicable international law'.

249 GHLPWP Report, *supra* note 15, at 31.

250 See also Principle 21 on reconstruction, rehabilitation and repair of water infrastructure and water-related infrastructure.

2.18 *Principle 18: Occupation*

The Occupying Power must restore and ensure public order and civil life in the occupied territory, including through the maintenance of water infrastructure and water-related infrastructure essential for the provision of water and sanitation services.

2.18.1 Commentary

1. The Occupying Power has an obligation to restore and ensure public order and safety and, unless absolutely prevented, respect the laws in force in the occupied territory.[251] This obligation has been interpreted as encompassing restoring and ensuring civil life, in line with the corresponding text of the French version of the Hague Regulations.[252] Accordingly, the Occupying Power should effectively administer the territory it occupies and ensure the continuation of normal public life and promote the welfare of the population under its control.[253] This obligation includes the operation and management, and if necessary, the reconstruction, rehabilitation or repair, of water infrastructure and water-related infrastructure indispensable for the public water and sanitation services.[254] Further, the Occupying Power has an obligation to ensure that the population under its control has necessary foodstuffs and other supplies essential to its survival.[255] It must also ensure and maintain 'the medical and hospital establishments and services, public health and hygiene in the occupied territory'.[256]

---

251 Hague Regulations, *supra* note 72, Art. 43. The Occupying Power may however, among others, 'legislate to fulfil its obligations under [Geneva Convention IV] or to enhance civil life in occupied territory'. T. Ferraro, (ed.), *Occupation and Other Forms of Administration of Foreign Territory* (Geneva: ICRC, 2012), at 58.

252 *Id.*, at 56–57.

253 See, for example, United Nations Security Council, '*Situation between Iraq and Kuwait*', 22 May 2003, UNSC Resolution 1483, UN Doc. S/RES/1483, para 4: 'Calls upon the Authority, consistent with the Charter of the United Nations and other relevant international law, to promote the welfare of the Iraqi people through the effective administration of the territory'.

254 See, for example, for the consequences of lack of electricity in the occupied Kuwait, United Nations Security Council, *Letter dated 26 April 1991 from the Secretary-General addressed to the President of the Security Council*, UN Doc S/22535 (29 April 1991), para 256: 'Virtually every sector of civic and social activities, such as water supply, sewerage, health care, education and water production is sustained by electricity. Its temporary absence in Kuwait has considerably retarded the re-establishment of normal life'.

255 Geneva Convention IV, *supra* note 35, Art. 55; Additional Protocol I, *supra* note 35, Art. 69(1).

256 Geneva Convention IV, *supra* note 35, Art. 56.

2. In the occupied territories, the Occupying Power must fulfil its obligations under international human rights law, including the International Covenant on Economic, Social and Cultural Rights.[257] At a minimum, it must meet its core obligations stemming from the right to water, including ensuring physical access to water facilities and services on a non-discriminatory basis.[258] If these services are already being provided by the local administration, it should not interfere with their operation and management of water infrastructure. If the Occupying Power cannot meet its core obligations and the basic needs of the civilian population, it must allow and facilitate humanitarian assistance.[259]

3. Under international humanitarian law, the Occupying Power must not destroy water infrastructure and water-related infrastructure unless required by imperative military necessity.[260] In particular, it must not destroy, remove or render useless the water infrastructure which contribute to the provision of water indispensable for the survival of the civilian population.[261] Similarly,

---

257 ICJ, Legal Consequences of the Construction of a Wall in the Occupied Palestinian Territory, Advisory Opinion, 9 July 2004, paras 106 and 112: '[T]he territories occupied by Israel have for over 37 years been subject to its territorial jurisdiction as the occupying Power. In the exercise of the powers available to it on this basis, Israel is bound by the provisions of the International Covenant on Economic, Social and Cultural Rights.'; ICJ, Case concerning Armed Activities on the Territory of the Congo (Democratic Republic of the Congo v. Uganda), Judgment, 19 December 2005, para 178: 'The Court thus concludes that Uganda was the occupying Power in Ituri at the relevant time. As such it was under an obligation, according to Article 43 of the Hague Regulations of 1907, to take all the measures in its power to restore, and ensure, as far as possible, public order and safety in the occupied area, while respecting, unless absolutely prevented, the laws in force in the DRC. This obligation comprised the duty to secure respect for the applicable rules of international human rights law'.

258 General Comment No. 15, *supra* note 45, para 37. See Principle 3 on the human rights to water and sanitation.

259 Geneva Convention IV, *supra* note 35, Art. 59. See also Principle 17 on humanitarian access and assistance.

260 ICRC Customary IHL Study, *supra* note 35, Rule 51; Geneva Convention IV, *supra* note 35, Art. 53. See also UN Commission on Human Rights, *Report on the Situation of Human Rights in Kuwait under Iraqi Occupation, prepared by Mr. Walter Kälin, Special Rapporteur of the Commission on Human Rights, in accordance with Commission resolution 1991/74*, Doc E/CN.4/1992/26 (16 January 1992), para 235: 'Many instances of confiscation, dismantling or destruction of infrastructure and of other public or private property, however, were deliberate, premeditated, systematic and large scale. They violated the guarantees of the Fourth Geneva Convention because they were not necessitated by military considerations nor were they otherwise admissible under international law'. The protection of water infrastructure as public or private property respectively will not be dealt with in this commentary.

261 Additional Protocol I, *supra* note 35, Art. 54(2). See, for example, UN Human Rights Council, *Report of the Special Rapporteur on the Situation of Human Rights in the*

under international human rights law, states must 'refrain from interfering directly or indirectly with the enjoyment of the right to water'.[262] Also related to this, the Occupying Power must not use its control over the water infrastructure to force the displacement of the civilian population outside the occupied territory, for example by retaining drinking water.[263]

4. The Occupying Power should carry out, as necessary, the reconstruction, rehabilitation and repair of water infrastructure and water-related infrastructure.[264] In the same vein, the Occupying Power should not arbitrarily deny or restrict the entry of equipment and other goods necessary for the reconstruction, rehabilitation, repair, operation and maintenance of water infrastructure and water-related infrastructure to the occupied territories.[265]

Palestinian Territories Occupied Since 1967, UN Doc A/HRC/40/73 (15 March 2019), para 26: 'A cluster of Palestinian villages in the South Hebron Hills have had their newly-laid water pipes, which had finally brought them clean running water, destroyed by the Israeli Civil Administration, forcing them to buy expensive trucked-in water for their homes and animals'. (Footnotes omitted.) See Principle 12 on starvation and water infrastructure indispensable to the survival of the civilian population.

262 General Comment No. 15, *supra* note 45, para 21: 'The obligation includes, *inter alia*, refraining from engaging in any practice or activity that denies or limits equal access to adequate water; arbitrarily interfering with customary or traditional arrangements for water allocation; unlawfully diminishing or polluting water, for example through waste from State-owned facilities or through use and testing of weapons; and limiting access to, or destroying, water services and infrastructure as a punitive measure, for example, during armed conflicts in violation of international humanitarian law'. See, for example, 'Report of the Special Rapporteur on the Palestinian Territories', *supra* note 261, para 52: '[S]ome Israeli settlements have taken control of Palestinian water springs in the West Bank with the assistance of the Israeli military. The Palestinians who have lost access to their springs often have no connection to water networks, and had relied upon the springs as their main or only source for drinking water and agricultural requirements' (footnotes omitted).

263 See, for example, UN Office for the Coordination of Humanitarian Affairs, '*Demolition and Seizure of Service Infrastructure in Palestinian Communities in Area C Exacerbates Risk of Forcible Transfer*', The Monthly Humanitarian Bulletin (September 2017). See also Principle 16 on forced displacement.

264 See, for example, UNSC Resolution 1483, *supra* note 253, para 14: 'Underlines that the Development Fund for Iraq shall be used in a transparent manner to meet the humanitarian needs of the Iraqi people, for the … repair of Iraq's infrastructure, … and for other purposes benefiting the people of Iraq'. See also Principle 21 on reconstruction, rehabilitation and repair of water infrastructure and water-related infrastructure.

265 Such restrictions can directly impede the return to, or the continuation of, the civil life in the occupied territories. See, for example, WHO, *Health Conditions in the Occupied Palestinian Territory, including East Jerusalem, and in the Occupied Syrian Golan*, UN Doc A70/39 (22 May 2017), para 24: 'Repair of 2014 damage to water and sanitation infrastructure, and implementation of long-term solutions, has been delayed due to restrictions on the import of necessary equipment and construction materials'.

5. The ILA has also addressed situations of occupation in its work related to water. The Madrid Rules stipulate that '[i]n occupied territories, seizure, destruction or intentional damage to water installations should be prohibited when their integral maintenance and effectiveness would be vital to the health and survival of the civilian population'.[266] With the same purpose, the Berlin Rules provide that the Occupying Power 'shall protect water installations and ensure an adequate water supply to the population of an occupied territory'.[267]

6. It should also be noted that, as the *de facto* authority, the Occupying Power must administer the natural resources of the occupied territory, including the water resources, in accordance with the rule of usufruct, without detriment to their capital.[268] Along similar lines, the ILA's Berlin Rules stipulate that the Occupying Power 'shall administer water resources in an occupied territory in a way that ensures the sustainable use of the water resources and that minimizes environmental harm'.[269] Furthermore, if there is a transboundary watercourse in the occupied territory, the Occupying Power should respect and fulfil any obligations stemming from customary international water law and transboundary watercourse agreements concluded prior to occupation.

7. Lastly, while this Principle and its commentary exclusively concern situations of occupation, the Geneva List urges that non-state parties to armed conflicts which have control over territory also follow these rules applicable to occupation and ensure that the civilian population under their control has access to water.

2.19 *Principle 19: Peace Agreements*

1. Peace agreements must not deprive peoples of their rights to water and sanitation.

---

266 Madrid Rules, *supra* note 32, Art. 6(3). See also ILA, '*International Water Resources Law*', Report of the Fifty-seventh Conference, Madrid, 30 August–4 September 1976 (London, 1978) 213–266, at 236: 'It is also unsatisfactory that ... Art. 56 para 2 of the Fourth Hague Convention ... does not give protection to water installations, although their integral maintenance and effectiveness may be vital to the health and the survival of the civilian population in occupied territories'.

267 Berlin Rules, *supra* note 32, Art. 54(2).

268 Hague Regulations, *supra* note 72, Art. 55. See also 'Report of the Special Rapporteur on the Palestinian Territories', *supra* note 261, para 42: 'Under the laws of occupation, groundwater is considered immovable public property, and its appropriation by the occupying power is restricted to normal use for military and administrative necessity' (footnotes omitted).

269 Berlin Rules, *supra* note 32, Art. 54(1). See also Madrid Rules, *supra* note 32, Art. 6(2): 'The occupying power should administer enemy property according to the indispensable requirements of the hydrologic balance'.

2. Peace agreements should be concluded in accordance with the principle of equitable and reasonable utilization of water resources.

2.19.1 Commentary

1. Peace agreements[270] concluded between state or non-state parties to an armed conflict cannot impede the realization of the human right to water or other human rights.[271] On the contrary, they should ensure the entire population's access to water and sanitation, including displaced persons and former combatants, whether they are returning home at the end of the conflict or remaining in refugee or displacement camps.[272] The ILA specifically refers to peace treaties and stipulates that they should not deprive 'a people of its water resources to such an extent that a threat to the health or to the economic or physical conditions of survival is created'.[273] Regarding water infrastructure, it states that '[w]hen, as the result of the fixing of a new frontier, the hydraulic system in the territory of one State is dependent on works established in the territory of another State, arrangements should be made for the safeguarding of uninterrupted delivery of water supplies indispensable for the vital needs of the people'.[274]

2. The right of states to an equitable and reasonable share of the natural resources should not be compromised by the conclusion of peace agreements.

---

270 For the purposes of this List, the term 'peace agreements' means all agreements concluded between the parties to a conflict, state or non-state, bringing an end to international and non-international armed conflict.

271 See General Comment No. 15, *supra* note 45, para 35: 'With regard to the conclusion and implementation of other international and regional agreements, States parties should take steps to ensure that these instruments do not adversely impact upon the right to water.'; para 31: 'To comply with their international obligations in relation to the right to water, States parties have to respect the enjoyment of the right in other countries. International cooperation requires States parties to refrain from actions that interfere, directly or indirectly, with the enjoyment of the right to water in other countries'. See also Common Article 1(2) of the International Covenant on Civil and Political Rights (16 December 1966) and ICESCR, *supra* note 45: 'All peoples may, for their own ends, freely dispose of their natural wealth and resources without prejudice to any obligations arising out of international economic co-operation, based upon the principle of mutual benefit, and international law. In no case may a people be deprived of its own means of subsistence'.

272 See, for example, the Darfur Peace Agreement (5 May 2006) concluded by the government of Sudan and the Sudan Liberation Movement, Art. 17, para 97; Final Agreement to End the Armed Conflict and Build a Stable and Lasting Peace (24 November 2016) between the National Government of Colombia and the Revolutionary Armed Forces of Colombia—People's Army (FARC-EP), Arts. 1.1.10, 1.3.2.3 [Colombia Peace Agreement].

273 Madrid Rules, *supra* note 32, Art. 8.

274 *Id.*

The protection and management of water infrastructure, especially that on transboundary watercourses and aquifers, should be regulated by peace agreements, in accordance with the principle of equitable and reasonable utilization of water resources and the obligation not to cause significant harm to other watercourse states or to the environment. These rules are codified in the UN Watercourses Convention[275] and recognized as customary law by the ICJ and other international tribunals.[276] The Geneva List encourages peace agreements between non-state parties to an armed conflict or a state and a non-state party, when relevant, to be concluded in accordance with the principle of equitable and reasonable sharing of natural resources.

3. The equitable and reasonable use of water resources includes the protection of ecosystems at both the domestic and transboundary levels. Rivers and aquifers must be managed sustainably. This reflects the need to balance economic, social, and environmental values in the use of water resources in line with the principle of sustainable development.[277] The ILA defines 'sustainable use' as the 'integrated management of resources to assure efficient use of and equitable access to waters for the benefit of current and future generations while preserving renewable resources and maintaining non-renewable resources to the maximum extent reasonably possible'.[278]

4. International practice also indicates that peace agreements are relevant for the peaceful management of transboundary watercourses. They may affirm the freedom of navigation for the contracting parties (riparian and non-riparian states) and the obligation to execute works for the benefit of navigation.[279]

---

275 UN Watercourses Convention, *supra* note 84, Arts 5, 7, 20. See also UNECE Convention, *supra* note 84, Article 2(1)–(2); ILC Draft Articles on Aquifers, *supra* note 84, Arts 4, 6, 12. These principles are also affirmed in a number of transboundary freshwater agreements (see, for example, Charter of Waters of the River Senegal (28 May 2002), Art. 4; Convention on Cooperation for the Protection and Sustainable Use of the Danube River (29 June 1994), Arts 2(1), 5(1); Agreement on the Cooperation for the Sustainable Development of the Mekong River Basin (5 April 1995), Arts 5, 7; Revised Protocol on Shared Watercourses in the Southern African Development Community (7 August 2000), Arts 3(10)(a), 4(2)(a), 4(2)(b)(i).

276 Gabčíkovo-Nagymaros Judgment, *supra* note 218, paras 53 and 85 (protection of the environment and principle of equitable and reasonable utilization); Nuclear Weapons Advisory Opinion, *supra* note 72, para 29 (obligation to respect the environment of other states or of areas beyond national control). See also Permanent Court of Arbitration, *Indus Water Kishenganga Arbitration* (*Islamic Republic of Pakistan v. Republic of India*), Final Award, 20 December 2013, paras 85, 87.

277 Gabčíkovo-Nagymaros Judgment, *supra* note 218, para 140.

278 Berlin Rules, *supra* note 32, Art. 3(19).

279 See, for example, Final Act of the Vienna Congress (9 June 1815), Arts. CIX (freedom of navigation), CXIII (towing paths), CXVII (confirmation of particular regulations

Some peace agreements establish joint commissions[280] or promote the conclusion of transboundary watercourse agreements.[281] It is recommended that peace agreements promote the conclusion of transboundary watercourse agreements and the joint management of water infrastructure. Agreements on transboundary water resources and joint management of water infrastructure both contribute to consolidating peace and preventing recurrence of violence.

5. Lastly, apart from its vital importance for people, the inclusion of water in peace agreements is also an important factor for a long-lasting peace.[282] Especially water infrastructure benefitting both sides of a conflict can be a confidence-building measure, contributing to the stability of peace.[283] Cooperation between the ex-belligerent parties on the reconstruction and management of water infrastructure likewise contributes to peacebuilding

respecting the navigation of the Rhine, the Neckar, the Maine, the Moselle, the Meuse, and the Scheldt); General Act of the Berlin Conference (26 February 1885), Arts XIII (freedom of navigation on the Congo River), XXVI (freedom of navigation on the Niger River).

280 See, for example, Treaty of Paris (30 March 1856), which established the Danube Commission to facilitate navigation on the river (Articles XV–XVII); Final Act of the Vienna Congress (9 June 1815), which created the current Central Commission for Navigation on the Rhine (Articles CVIII and CXVII). This Commission has also been the subject of the Treaty of Versailles (28 June 1919) (Part XII, Chapter IV, Arts 354–362). See, for a recent example, Annex II (Water Related Matters) to the Treaty of Peace between the Hashemite Kingdom of Jordan and the State of Israel (26 October 1994), Article 7, which provides for a Joint Water Committee.

281 See, for example, Treaty of Peace with Turkey (24 July 1923), para 109: 'In default of any provisions to the contrary, when as the result of the fixing of a new frontier the hydraulic system (canalization, inundation, irrigation, drainage or similar matters) in a State is dependent on works executed within the territory of another State, or when use is made on the territory of a State, in virtue of pre-war usage, of water or hydraulic power, the source of which is on the territory of another State, an agreement shall be made between the States concerned to safeguard the interests and rights acquired by each of them'.

282 GWH Report, *supra* note 11, at 11.

283 See, for example, 'Enguri / Vardnili Hydro Power Cascade Rehabilitation', on file with the authors, cited in the Geneva List of Principles on the Protection of Water Infrastructure, August 2019, at 84: 'The project concerns the preparation and implementation of the last stage of rehabilitation (phase III) of the Enguri hydro-power plant and the Vardnili Cascade. Built in the 1970's and located in North West Georgia on both sides of the border with the breakaway region of Abkhazia, these were partly destroyed during the civil war in 1995. Enguri HPP supplies around half of the electricity consumed in Georgia and is an essential part of the Caucasus energy system.... The project can also be seen as an element of stability in Southern Abkhazia and as a confidence-building measure'. Other examples include the Diama Dam on the Senegal River at the border between Senegal and Mauritania. These two countries were parties to an armed conflict due to a border dispute between 1989 and 1991.

and preventing the reoccurrence of violence.[284] For example, in Georgia, it has been reported that working together on a water supply for mutual benefit had a positive impact on the relations among villages that had experienced tensions.[285]

2.20 *Principle 20: Joint Mechanisms and Commissions*

Watercourse States should create joint mechanisms and commissions, or in any case cooperate and coordinate, with a view to ensuring the protection, safe operation and maintenance of water infrastructure located on transboundary water resources.

2.20.1 Commentary

1. It is clear that having states negotiate and conclude agreements with their opponents during armed conflicts poses difficulties. States are thus encouraged to conclude agreements on the protection of water infrastructure during peacetime.[286] Before going further into the practice relating to joint

---

284 See, for example, the contribution to lasting peace of the International Sava River Basin Commission, established by the Framework Agreement on the Sava River Basin (3 December 2002) referred to in A. Čolakhodžić, M. Filipović, J. Kovandžić & S. Stec, '*The Sava River: Transitioning to peace in the former Yugoslavia*' in E. Weinthal, J. Troell & M. Nakayaman (eds.), *Water and Post-Conflict Peacebuilding* (London: Earthscan, 2013) 271–296.

285 Organization for Security and Co-operation in Europe, Mission to Georgia, *Economic Rehabilitation Works*, Issue 1 (Tbilisi: OSCE, 2008), at 35. See also at 34: 'As well as improving the day-to-day situation for people living in villages, the regular supply of drinking water to an area can build confidence between neighbouring villages by removing one possible source of dispute'.

286 Regarding transboundary water resources, see UNECE Convention, *supra* note 84, Article 9: '1. The Riparian Parties shall on the basis of equality and reciprocity enter into bilateral or multilateral agreements or other arrangements, where these do not yet exist, or adapt existing ones, where necessary to eliminate the contradictions with the basic principles of this Convention, in order to define their mutual relations and conduct regarding the prevention, control and reduction of transboundary impact.... 2. The agreements or arrangements mentioned in paragraph 1 of this article shall provide for the establishment of joint bodies'. See also UN Watercourses Convention, *supra* note 84, Article 8(2): '[W]atercourse States may consider the establishment of joint mechanisms or commissions, as deemed necessary by them, to facilitate cooperation on relevant measures and procedures in the light of experience gained through cooperation in existing joint mechanisms and commissions in various regions' and Article 24: '1. Watercourse States shall, at the request of any of them, enter into consultations concerning the management of an international watercourse, which may include the establishment of a joint management mechanism. 2. For the purposes of this article, 'management' refers, in particular, to: (a) planning the sustainable development of an international watercourse and providing for the implementation of any plans adopted; and (b) otherwise promoting

mechanisms and commissions, it should be remembered that Additional Protocol I urges the parties to conclude further agreements with a view to providing additional protection for objects containing dangerous forces, such as dams and dykes, which may also be on transboundary watercourses.[287] In addition to this, states sharing watercourses are encouraged to conclude further agreements conferring protection, additional to that already provided by international humanitarian law, to all installations on the shared watercourses.

2. Joint mechanisms or commissions can continue working during armed conflicts and serve as a means of communication between the parties to the conflict. For example, the Permanent Indus Commission, established under the Indus Waters Treaty between India and Pakistan, has maintained its work through armed conflicts between the states since its establishment in 1960.[288] The Organization for the Development of the Senegal River (in French *Organisation pour la mise en valeur du Fleuve Senegal* (OMVS)), on the other hand, not only continued its work during the conflict between Mauritania and Senegal, but also had a role in reinitiating the diplomatic ties between the two countries.[289] Consequently, these mechanisms can provide a much needed fora of dialogue between belligerent states and have the potential to foster the protection of water infrastructure.[290]

3. After an armed conflict, it is recommended that the parties to the conflict rebuild water management schemes, especially irrigation and drinking water plans, and implement environmental protection programmes.[291] Priority should be given to the rehabilitation of the environment and reconstruction of governance mechanisms. For example, the peace agreement between the

rational and optimal utilization, protection and control of the watercourse.'; ILC Draft Articles on Aquifers, *supra* note 84, Art. 14.

287 Additional Protocol I, *supra* note 35, Art. 56(6). See Principle 13 on water infrastructure containing dangerous forces.

288 The purpose and functions of the Permanent Indus Commission include serving as a channel of communication and promoting co-operation between the parties in the developments of the waters of the rivers. Indus Waters Treaty (16 September 1960), Art. 8(1)–(2).

289 A. Grzybowski, *Innovations in Trans-boundary Water Management: Pacific Resolutions* (UN Regional Centre for Preventive Diplomacy for Central Asia, 2013), at 20–21.

290 See also ILC, *Third Report on the Protection of the Environment in Relation to Armed Conflicts Submitted by Marie G. Jacobsson, Special Rapporteur*, Doc A/CN.4/700 (3 June 2016), para 150: 'The joint mechanisms and commissions provide an additional example of possibilities for cooperation and trust building in the context of shared resources. Improving water governance has been used as a tool for mitigating tension and hostilities in several different contexts, such as, for example [*sic*] in Liberia, Afghanistan and Nigeria' (footnotes omitted).

291 See also Principle 19 on peace agreements.

National Government of Colombia and the Revolutionary Armed Forces of Colombia—People's Army (FARC-EP) points out that the government 'will set up and implement the National Irrigation and Drainage Plan (Plan Nacional de Riego y Drenaje) for the rural, family-run and community-based economies'.[292]

2.21 *Principle 21: Reconstruction, Rehabilitation and Repair of Water Infrastructure and Water-Related Infrastructure*

1. Destroyed and damaged water infrastructure and water-related infrastructure should be reconstructed, rehabilitated and repaired.
2. The equipment and other goods necessary for the reconstruction, rehabilitation, repair, operation and maintenance of water infrastructure and water-related infrastructure should be exempted from sanctions and other coercive measures.

2.21.1 Commentary

1. It is primarily the responsibility of the territorial sovereign state to provide the civilian population with its basic needs of survival, and as such to carry out the reconstruction, rehabilitation and repair of the water infrastructure that contribute to the satisfaction of their basic needs. Reconstruction, rehabilitation and repair of damaged or destroyed water infrastructure, especially those which provide drinking and irrigation water, is a pressing issue both during and in the aftermath of armed conflicts. This infrastructure is crucial for the fulfilment of the right to life and other human rights of people living in previous conflict zones and for the safe and dignified return of refugees and internally displaced persons.[293] In particular, returnees' access to water should be ensured if needed through the reconstruction, rehabilitation and repair of

292 Colombia Peace Agreement, *supra* note 272, Art. 1.3.1.2; see also Darfur Peace Agreement, *supra* note 272, Art. 17.

293 *Centre of Housing Rights and Evictions v. The Sudan*, African Commission on Human and People's Rights, 279/03–296/05 (2009), para 229(5): 'The African Commission recommends that the Respondent State should take all necessary and urgent measures to ensure protection of victims of human rights violations in the Darfur Region, including to … rehabilitate economic and social infrastructure, such as education, health, water, and agricultural services, in the Darfur provinces in order to provide conditions for return in safety and dignity for the IDPs and Refugees'. See also European Union, Delegation to Georgia, 'EU Assistance to People Affected by Conflict in Georgia', Overview (2011), at 15: 'The rehabilitation of basic infrastructure in the conflict-affected areas represents an essential element for the economic rehabilitation, as well as the safe and dignified repatriation of refugees and displaced persons'.

water infrastructure.[294] A failure to provide the basic services adds to the vulnerability of the population recovering from an armed conflict.

2. Comprehensive water infrastructure and water-related infrastructure damage assessments, including the identification of the impact of the damage on people and the environment, should be conducted following the end of armed conflicts.[295] These assessments should inform the reconstruction, rehabilitation and repair strategies for ensuring access to water and ultimately be carried out with a view to attaining lasting peace. Indeed, these works should not only be directed at fulfilling the short-term needs of the population, but also take into consideration their long-term effects.[296] The reconstruction planning process should take into account the new realities or changed needs of the local population in the aftermath of the armed conflict and be inclusive of all segments of the society, not leaving out marginalized groups or minorities.

3. Areas where the water infrastructure is located may be contaminated with war remnants after the end of conflict.[297] States must clear the surroundings

294 See in general on 'enabling return through the realization of the human rights to water and sanitation', Report of the Special Rapporteur on the Human Rights to Safe Drinking Water and Sanitation, *supra* note 26, paras 51–52.

295 The work of Post-Conflict and Disaster Management Branch of UNEP can be of guidance in carrying out these assessments. See, for example, their assessment of the environmental impacts of the Sudanese conflict, UNEP, *Sudan: Post-Conflict Environmental Assessment* (Nairobi: UNEP, 2007), at 70–97. See also Parliamentary Assembly of the Council of Europe, *Economic Reconstruction and Renewal in South-eastern Europe following the Kosovo Conflict, Addendum to the Report*, Doc 8503 (16 September 1999), para 5: 'The staff of the UN Interim Administration Mission in Kosovo (UNMIK) responsible for the so-called "Pillar 4" (Economic Reconstruction and Development) are now preparing a detailed damage assessment (infrastructure, energy, housing, etc.) for the second Donors' Conference to be held in October 1999'.

296 See UNICEF, Water Under Fire, *supra* note 9. It should also be noted that hasty measures may also have negative impacts. See, for example, O. Macharis & N. Farajalla, *Case Study on the 2006 Israel-Lebanon War and its Impact on Water Resources and Water Infrastructure in Lebanon* (on file with the authors): 'The haste of reconstruction however, prompted the random dumping of large amounts of demolition waste, including in watercourses, which led to the deterioration of water quality due to the obstruction of river flows and the creation of stagnant pools of water. Some of the rubble was also dumped in the sea along the Ouzai highway leading out of the southern suburbs of Beirut, leading to land reclamation and seawater pollution'.

297 See, for example, *id.*: 'Because of the heavy bombardments during the conflict, Lebanon was contaminated by large quantities of unexploded aerial bombs, missiles, rockets, cluster munitions, artillery shells and mortar bombs.... Importantly, the presence of these by-products of war constitutes an important barrier to early recovery efforts, obstructing the reestablishment of the most essential services. Restoring water pipes for instance, is impossible until the unexploded ordnances are removed and the contaminated areas are cleared'.

of the water infrastructure from all explosive and toxic remnants of war to prevent, or in any case mitigate, environmental pollution. They must comply with their obligations under disarmament law to ensure people's access to water and reconstruction teams' access to water infrastructure.[298]

4. Sanctions and coercive measures[299] against states that are involved in or recovering from an armed conflict may have a negative impact on the population of the targeted states.[300] They can unintendedly deny the population of its basic needs due to restrictions on imports of spare parts and chemicals required for maintaining essential services such as water and sanitation. The issue becomes more complicated when these critical inputs for the infrastructure, such as cement, piping, electrical equipment or chemical substances, can potentially be used for other, military, purposes. In May 2002, with a view to improving the humanitarian situation in Iraq, new procedures were set in place by the UN Security Council for the processing of contracts for humanitarian supplies,[301] and, since then, the Council has in certain contexts provided for humanitarian exceptions for sanctions.[302]

298 Protocol II to the CCW, *supra* note 140, Art. 3(2); Convention on the Prohibition of the Use, Stockpiling, Production and Transfer of Anti-Personnel Mines (18 September 1997), Art. 5(1); Convention on Cluster Munitions (30 May 2008), Art. 4(1). See also ILC, *Protection of the Environment in Relation to Armed Conflict, supra* note 20, Draft Principle 27.

299 Sanctions normally refer to measures enacted by the Security Council acting under Chapter VII of the Charter of the UN. For the purposes of the Geneva List, the term 'coercive measures' refers to all other measures taken by states or international organizations.

300 UN Committee on Economic, Social and Cultural Rights, 'General Comment No. 8: The relationship between economic sanctions and respect for economic, social and cultural rights' (1997), para 3: '[Sanctions] often cause significant disruption in the distribution of food, pharmaceuticals and sanitation supplies, jeopardize the quality of food and the availability of clean drinking water, severely interfere with the functioning of basic health and education systems, and undermine the right to work'.

301 United Nations Security Council, '*Situation between Iraq and Kuwait*', 14 May 2002, UNSC Resolution 1409, UN Doc. S/RES/1409.

302 See, for example, United Nations Security Council, '*Libya*', 16 September 2011, UNSC Resolution 2009, UN Doc. S/RES/2009, para 16 for the exceptions of sanctions against Libya: 'Decides that in addition to the provisions of paragraph 19 of resolution 1970 (2011), the measures imposed ... do not apply to funds, other financial assets or economic resources of the Central Bank of Libya, the LAFB, the LIA and the LAIP provided that: (a) a Member State has provided notice to the Committee of its intent to authorize access to funds, other financial assets, or economic resources, for one or more of the following purposes and in the absence of a negative decision by the Committee within five working days of such a notification: (i) humanitarian needs; (ii) fuel, electricity and water for strictly civilian uses; ... (iv) establishing, operating, or strengthening institutions of civilian government and civilian public infrastructure'.

5. Sanctions and coercive measures should be designed in a manner that takes into account their possible negative impact on the population, including due to delays in, or impossibility of, the repair, rehabilitation or reconstruction of water infrastructure.[303] They should also refrain from imposing measures that would interfere with the provision of goods essential for access to water.[304] In particular, equipment and spare parts necessary for the repair of water infrastructure and chemical substances necessary for the treatment of water, such as chlorine, and their financing should be exempted from the scope of sanctions and other coercive measures. Any unilateral measure implemented by states should 'be imposed no longer than necessary, be proportional and be subject to appropriate human rights safeguards, including human rights impact assessments and monitoring conducted by independent experts'.[305] States should also 'ensure effective exemptions for satisfying basic human rights and essential humanitarian needs'.[306]

2.22 *Principle 22: Peacekeeping Operations*

1. Protection of water infrastructure and water-related infrastructure and their reconstruction, rehabilitation and repair should be included in the mandates of the peacekeeping operations, where appropriate.

---

303 See General Comment No. 8, *supra* note 300, para 4: 'In considering sanctions, it is essential to distinguish between the basic objective of applying political and economic pressure upon the governing élite of the country to persuade them to conform to international law, and the collateral infliction of suffering upon the most vulnerable groups within the targeted country'. See also regarding the humanitarian situation in Iraq aggravated by the sanctions, United Nations Security Council, *Report of the Second Panel Established Pursuant to the Note by the President of the Security Council of 30 January 1999 (S/1999/100), Concerning the Current Humanitarian Situation in Iraq*, UN Doc S/1999/356 (30 March 1999), Annex II, para 45: 'Even if not all suffering in Iraq can be imputed to external factors, especially sanctions, the Iraqi people would not be undergoing such deprivations in the absence of the prolonged measures imposed by the Security Council and the effects of war'.

304 General Comment No. 15, *supra* note 45, para 32.

305 UN Human Rights Council, *Thematic Study of the Office of the United Nations High Commissioner for Human Rights on the Impact of Unilateral Coercive Measures on the Enjoyment of Human Rights, including Recommendations on Actions Aimed at Ending Such Measures*, UN Doc A/HRC/19/33 (11 January 2012), para 38. These criteria are set forth within the context of discussions regarding sanctions imposed to end gross human rights violations.

306 UN Human Rights Council, *Report of the Special Rapporteur on the Negative Impact of Unilateral Coercive Measures on the Enjoyment of Human Rights*, UN Doc A/HRC/36/44 (26 July 2017), Appendix II, Elements for a draft General Assembly declaration on unilateral coercive measures and the rule of law, para 13(b).

2. Peacekeeping operations should support and provide assistance to the local authorities in the reconstruction, rehabilitation, repair, operation and maintenance of the water infrastructure and water-related infrastructure.

2.22.1 Commentary

1. The mandates of peacekeeping operations should include the protection of water infrastructure and water-related infrastructure, with a view to ensuring access to basic services.[307] This inclusion in their mandates should allow for their reconstruction, rehabilitation and repair, along with their protection, safe operation and management.

2. The mandates of UN peacekeeping operations have evolved over the years to encompass a wide range of activities related to peace and security. Today these operations include different objectives, including the protection of civilians.[308] Peacekeeping operations often operate in environments where water infrastructure is minimal or severely degraded. In these situations, the deployment of water specialists in peace operations to rehabilitate and rebuild water supply systems should be encouraged.[309] The UN peacekeeping missions should collaborate with other UN agencies, such as the UN Development Programme and the World Health Organization (WHO) and draw upon their respective expertise.[310]

307 For the purposes of the Geneva List, 'peacekeeping operations' mean those operations established by the UN as well as by other organizations, such as NATO or the African Union.

308 UNGA, *Report of the High-Level Independent Panel on Peace on Uniting our Strengths for Peace: Politics, Partnership and People*, UN Doc A/70/95 (17 June 2015), paras 82–85.

309 GHLPWP Report, *supra* note 15, at 31.

310 For example, the collapse of water infrastructure can have effects on both the operation of health facilities and the public health. Their reparation can thus be crucial for the work of the WHO and this issue has been addressed in the Organization's work (WHO, Regional Office for the Eastern Mediterranean, *Reconstruction of the Afghanistan Health Sector: A Preliminary Assessment of Needs and Opportunities* (Cairo: WHO, 2002), para 6.3.4). See also General Comment No. 15, *supra* note 45, para 60: 'United Nations agencies and other international organizations concerned with water, such as [WHO, Food and Agriculture Organization of the UN, UNICEF, UNEP, UN Human Settlements Programme, International Labour Organization, UN Development Programme], the International Fund for Agricultural Development, as well as international organizations concerned with trade such as the World Trade Organization, should cooperate effectively with States parties, building on their respective expertise, in relation to the implementation of the right to water at the national level'.

3. Some infrastructure-related elements have already been integrated in the mandates of UN peacekeeping operations.[311] Missions have also taken up water infrastructure-related activities in practice. For example, the UN Mission in South Sudan has been involved in the operation of wastewater treatment plants[312] and the UN Stabilization Mission in Haiti has supported the improvement of water and sanitation infrastructure.[313] Other missions have carried out similar work through quick impact projects. For example, the UN Mission in South Sudan has provided drinking water systems,[314] and the UN Mission in Ethiopia and Eritrea has built simple water infrastructure through these projects.[315]

4. The peacekeeping operations should assist the local governments in fulfilling their essential state functions, including restoring basic services, with a view to consolidating peace and eliminating the possibility of a recurrence of violence.[316] To this end, the UN or other international organizations undertaking peacekeeping operations should cooperate with the local authorities and

311 See, for example, United Nations Security Council, '*Kosovo*', 10 June 1244, UNSC Resolution 1244, UN Doc. S/RES/1244, para 11: 'Decides that the main responsibilities of the international civil presence [UN Mission in Kosovo] will include: … (g) Supporting the reconstruction of key infrastructure and other economic reconstruction'. See also, UN Mission in Kosovo, Regulation No. 2000/49 on the Establishment of the Administrative Department of Public Utilities, UNMIK/REG/2000/49 (19 August 2000), para 1.2: 'The Department shall be responsible for the management oversight and regulation of matters relating to public utilities in Kosovo that shall include … water supply and waste water and solid waste collection and treatment, as may be provided by public, private and other enterprises and institutions providing such services'. See, for an example from a special political mission, United Nations Security Council, '*The situation in Libya*', 13 September 2018, UNSC Resolution 2434, UN Doc. S/RES/2434, para 2: 'Further decides that [UN Support Mission in Libya], within operational and security constraints, should undertake the following tasks: … (ii) support, on request, for the provision of essential services, and delivery of humanitarian assistance and in accordance with humanitarian principles'.

312 UNEP, *Greening the Blue Helmets: Environment, Natural Resources and UN Peacekeeping Operations* (Nairobi: UNEP, 2012), at 26.

313 UN Department of Public Information, *UN Peace Operations: Year in Review* (2012), at 12.

314 *Id.*, at 28.

315 UN Department of Public Information, *UN Peace Operations: Year in Review* (2004), at 13.

316 See, for an example from a peacebuilding office, United Nations Security Council, '*Central African Republic*', 28 January 2014, UNSC Resolution 2134, UN Doc. S/RES/2134, para 2: 'Decides that the mandate of [UN Integrated Peacebuilding Office in the Central African Republic] shall be reinforced and updated as follows: … (c) Extension of State authority: to promote and support the rapid restoration of state authority over the whole territory of the country; to assist [Central African Republic's] governmental institutions, including through technical assistance, to increase their capacity to perform basic government functions and deliver basic services to the Central African people'.

communities, enhancing their capacity in the repair and managing of water infrastructure.[317] In this way they can hand over the management of the water infrastructure to well-trained communities or authorities.[318] It is also of importance that the water infrastructure reconstruction, rehabilitation and repair projects can provide the population, including ex-combatants, with employment opportunities and serve as a foundation for economic recovery.[319]

2.23 *Principle 23: Martens Clause*

> In cases not covered by international agreements, water infrastructure and water-related infrastructure remain under the protection and authority of the principles of international law derived from established custom, the principles of humanity and the dictates of public conscience.

2.23.1 Commentary

1. The Martens Clause sets forth an overarching rule that even in the absence of specific treaty rules applicable to a certain situation, persons affected by armed conflicts are not 'completely deprived of protection'.[320] Indeed, it rebuts the assumption that 'anything which is not prohibited … is therefore permitted'.[321] This rule is reproduced in the Additional Protocols,[322] and is of customary nature.[323]

2. The emergence of the Martens Clause was in the Hague Convention II.[324] However, its content has also influenced documents other than those relating to

317 For example, the UN Mission in Liberia has supported local jobs and capacity-building through the rehabilitation and ongoing maintenance of Liberia's water infrastructure. UNEP, *supra* note 312, at 25.

318 *Id.*, at 24: '[UN Mission in Liberia] has also supported … capacity-building through the rehabilitation and ongoing maintenance of the host country's water infrastructure. At the closure of a mission, UN water infrastructure can also be handed over to local communities or host country water agencies, provided they are properly trained and have access to spare parts'.

319 There are examples of such experience in Sudan and Liberia (*Id.*, at 66).

320 M. Sassòli, A. Bouvier & A. Quintin (eds.), 'Martens Clause', *How Does Law Protect in War?, Online Casebook 2.0* (ICRC, 2014), https://casebook.icrc.org/glossary/martens-clause, accessed 12 June 2020.

321 ICRC Commentary, *supra* note 1, para 55.

322 Additional Protocol I, *supra* note 35, Art. 1(2); Additional Protocol II, *supra* note 35, Preamble.

323 Nuclear Weapons Advisory Opinion, *supra* note 72, para 84.

324 Hague Convention II, *supra* note 35, Preamble.

international humanitarian law.[325] Importantly, the Commentary of the ILC to Article 29 of the UN Watercourses Convention affirms this principle's application in case of a conflict between uses of an international watercourse, giving special consideration to the requirements of vital human needs.[326] Further, its relevance for the protection of the environment is demonstrated by the principle's inclusion in the Guidelines for Military Manuals and Instructions on the Protection of the Environment in Times of Armed Conflict drafted by the ICRC.[327]

3. The significance of this Clause for the purposes of the Geneva List is that while the water infrastructure and water-related infrastructure are protected by the rules and principles of international law, in the absence of a treaty rule applicable to a specific situation, they are not void of protection; they remain protected by the principles of international law derived from established custom, the principles of humanity and the dictates of public conscience.

2.24 *Principle 24: Implementation*

1. States must incorporate in their domestic frameworks their obligations relating to the protection of water infrastructure stemming from international law, as applicable.
2. States must implement in their domestic frameworks international crimes relating to the protection of water infrastructure, as applicable.
3. States are encouraged to incorporate in their domestic frameworks the recommendations of the Geneva List.

---

325 See, for example, Colombia Peace Agreement, *supra* note 272, Preamble: 'Accepting that customary international legal standards will continue to govern issues relating to fundamental rights not mentioned in the new Final Agreement, including the imperative whereby "in those cases not provided for by current law, the individual will be safeguarded by humanitarian principles and the demands of the public conscience"'.

326 ILC Draft Articles on Watercourses, *supra* note 154, Commentary to Article 29, para 3: 'In cases not covered by a specific rule, certain fundamental protections are afforded by the "Martens clause".... In essence, it provides that even in cases not covered by specific international agreements, civilians and combatants remain under the protection and authority of the principles of international law derived from established custom, from the principles of humanity and from the dictates of public conscience. The same general principle is expressed in article 10 of the draft articles [on the relationship between different kinds of uses], which provides that in reconciling a conflict between uses of an international watercourse, special attention is to be paid to the requirements of vital human needs' (footnotes omitted).

327 ICRC Environment Guidelines, *supra* note 207, para 7.

2.24.1 Commentary

1. States must incorporate in their domestic frameworks all rules of international humanitarian law,[328] international water law and international environmental law relating to the protection of water infrastructure, as applicable. In line with their obligations stemming from international human rights law, they should also adopt measures towards the full realization of the rights to water and sanitation, among others.[329] States are also encouraged to implement the principles of the Geneva List on the protection of water infrastructure in their domestic frameworks, where they go beyond their obligations stemming from international law. The term domestic framework is inclusive of, among others, national legislation, administrative rules and military manuals, training, doctrines and regulations.

2. States must also implement in their domestic frameworks international crimes relating to the protection of water infrastructure, as applicable. It is beyond the scope of the Geneva List to go into the detail of every international crime that might involve water infrastructure. For example, launching an attack against or otherwise damaging water infrastructure in the knowledge that incidental civilian harm 'would be excessive in relation to the concrete and direct military advantage anticipated' constitutes a grave breach of Additional Protocol I and a war crime in international armed conflicts under the Statute of the International Criminal Court (ICC).[330] Furthermore, attacks against water infrastructure indispensable to the survival of the civilian population can constitute one of the underlying acts of crimes against humanity and genocide.[331]

3. Here the Geneva List confines itself to setting forth two war crimes that particularly concern water infrastructure. First, launching an attack against works or installations containing dangerous forces, in the knowledge that

328 Importantly, states have an obligation to respect and ensure respect for international humanitarian law. See Common Article 1 of the four Geneva Conventions of 1949.

329 See ICESCR, *supra* note 45, Art. 2(1): 'Each State Party to the present Covenant undertakes to take steps, individually and through international assistance and co-operation, especially economic and technical, to the maximum of its available resources, with a view to achieving progressively the full realization of the rights recognized in the present Covenant by all appropriate means, including particularly the adoption of legislative measures'. See also General Comment No. 15, *supra* note 45, para 45.

330 Additional Protocol I, *supra* note 35, Art. 85(3)(b); Rome Statute of the International Criminal Court (17 July 1998), Art. 8(2)(b)(iv). The wording of the Rome Statute differs from that of Additional Protocol I, which is reproduced above, and includes a reference to damage to the environment.

331 International Criminal Court, Office of the Prosecutor, 'Annex A to the Public Redacted Version of the Prosecutor's Application under Article 58 (Situation in Darfur, the Sudan)' (2008), paras 172–176.

such attack will cause excessive loss of life, injury to civilians or damage to civilian objects, constitutes a grave breach of Additional Protocol I.[332] Second, intentionally using starvation of civilians as a method of warfare by depriving them of objects indispensable to their survival is a war crime under the Statute of the ICC when committed during an international armed conflict.[333] In December 2019, the Swiss proposal to make this a war crime punishable before the ICC when committed in non-international armed conflicts was unanimously accepted by the ICC Assembly of State Parties.[334] These two crimes cover the attacks directed against most water infrastructure, including dams, dykes, drinking water installations and irrigation works. Using starvation as a method of warfare is also listed as a customary war crime both in international and non-international armed conflicts by the ICRC Customary IHL Study, while launching attacks against works and installations containing dangerous forces may constitute a war crime only in international armed conflicts.[335] The Geneva List encourages states to criminalize these acts also when committed within the context of non-international armed conflicts.

3 Perspectives

The writing of this monograph coincides with the coronavirus disease outbreak (COVID-19) and the drastic measures taken against the pandemic by states around the globe. In this context, one of the main recommendations of the WHO for the general public is to wash their hands frequently.[336] However, it was reported in 2019 that '[s]ome 2.2 billion people around the world do not have safely managed drinking water services, 4.2 billion people do not have safely managed sanitation services, and 3 billion lack basic handwashing facilities'.[337] UN-Habitat warned that COVID-19 could take a heavier toll on urban slums.[338] While the world's leading humanitarian organizations are

332 Additional Protocol I, *supra* note 35, Art. 85(3)(c).

333 Rome Statute, *supra* note 330, Art. 8(2)(b)(xxv).

334 Switzerland, Federal Department of Foreign Affairs, 'Swiss Initiative: Intentional starvation of civilians in civil wars is now a war crime', Press release (6 December 2019).

335 ICRC Customary IHL Study, *supra* note 35, Rule 156.

336 WHO, *Coronavirus Disease (COVID-19) Advice for the Public*, https://www.who.int/emergencies/diseases/novel-coronavirus-2019/advice-for-public, accessed 12 June 2020.

337 World Bank, *Water*, https://www.worldbank.org/en/topic/water/overview, accessed 12 June 2020. See also UNICEF and WHO, *Progress on Household Drinking Water, Sanitation and Hygiene 2000–2017: Special Focus on Inequalities* (New York: UNICEF and WHO, 2019).

338 UN News, *Water Access Critical to Beating Back COVID-19 Spread in Slum Areas* (23 March 2020), https://news.un.org/en/story/2020/03/1060042?utm_source=UN+News

trying to take emergency measures to ensure access to water in vulnerable communities in urban settings or in refugee camps, we are reminded of the importance of uninterrupted and sustainable water provision to households and medical facilities.

Armed conflicts exacerbate the existing problems of access to basic water and sanitation services in places where the water infrastructure is already in poor condition. How heavily conflict affected countries such as Syria and Yemen will be able to respond to this pandemic is yet to be seen. However, it has already been reported that the civilians are put 'at unacceptable risk' by parties to the conflicts who are not renouncing their tactics of weaponizing water infrastructure during the spread of the disease.[339] Moreover, the dramatic impact of the spread of this infectious disease in conflict affected areas prompted the UN General-Secretary to call for a global ceasefire to reduce the risk of devastating losses in these countries.[340]

With the development of the Geneva List, the present authors, thanks to the support of the GWH, have tried to respond to the need to strengthen the protection of water infrastructure during and after armed conflicts as highlighted in the report of the Global High-Level Panel on Water and Peace.[341] As we have touched upon in the introduction, states are at best unenthusiastic about concluding new multilateral treaties. However, this should not discourage efforts towards better protection of water and water infrastructure. Soft law instruments and, more importantly, state practice that goes beyond the existing law, as demonstrated by the Geneva List, prove that even in the absence of a binding instrument, which would with no doubt be the most desirable option, there is a possibility for improvement.

+-+Newsletter&utm_campaign=6e84b77436-EMAIL_CAMPAIGN_2020_03_24_12_35&utm_medium=email&utm_term=0_fdbfiaf606-6e84b77436-105802149, accessed 12 June 2020.

339 UNICEF, 'Interruption to Key Water Station in the Northeast of Syria Puts 460,000 People at Risk as Efforts Ramp Up to Prevent the Spread of Coronavirus Disease', Statement (23 March 2020), https://www.unicef.org/press-releases/interruption-key-water-station-northeast-syria-puts-460000-people-risk-efforts-ramp, accessed 12 June 2020; Human Rights Watch, *Turkey/Syria: Weaponizing Water in Global Pandemic?* (31 March 2020), https://www.hrw.org/news/2020/03/31/turkey/syria-weaponizing-water-global-pandemic (accessed 12 June 2020).

340 United Nations Secretary-General, *Secretary-General's Appeal for Global Ceasefire* (23 March 2020), https://www.un.org/sg/en/content/sg/statement/2020-03-23/secretary-generals-appeal-for-global-ceasefire, accessed 12 June 2020.

341 GHLPWP Report, *supra* note 15, at 31.

3.1 *Challenges Ahead*

Today, any issue relating to natural resources, including water, cannot be discussed without considering climate change. The risks posed by climate change to water infrastructure in peacetime have already been documented.[342] While water sustainability is traditionally associated with environmental and development actors, humanitarian organizations working exclusively or mainly in conflict and other fragile contexts are also reflecting on the relationship between risks stemming from climate change and the need to adapt their operations to the impacts of climate change.[343] At the 33rd International Conference of the Red Cross and Red Crescent, which took place in December 2019, the International Federation of Red Cross and Red Crescent Societies and the ICRC pledged to strengthen 'the resilience of communities to climate change and environmental degradation through climate-smart humanitarian action'.[344]

The prophecies of water conflicts of the 1990s—conflicts which would have water as their sole trigger as opposed to one of several causes—were debunked in the 2000s.[345] However, the ever-escalating consequences of climate change, which put more and more stress on freshwater resources, may reverse the situation. Clear linkages have already been established between the effects of climate change on the environment in general and, for example, the armed conflicts in Darfur and Somalia.[346] Moreover, even the triggering of the armed conflict in Syria in 2011 was linked to increased prices of food

342 UN Water and UN Educational, Scientific and Cultural Organization (UNESCO), *The United Nations World Water Development Report 2020: Water and Climate Change* (Paris: UNESCO, 2020), at 48.

343 See, for example, C. Lune-Grayson, '*When Rain Turns to Dust: Climate Change, Conflict and Humanitarian Action*', Humanitarian Law and Policy (5 December 2019), https://blogs.icrc.org/law-and-policy/2019/12/05/rain-dust-climate-change-humanitarian-action/?utm_campaign=DP%20Forum%20-%20When%20rain%20turns%20to%20dust%3A%20climate%20change%20and%20humanitarian%20action&utm_source=hs_email&utm_medium=email&utm_content=80362163&_hsenc=p2ANqtz-90AyUbx1N7PpI6NqO7O2PWg8aJbQzWzuRik_dj93DFQHq2XgRkufkN1Wq8qMCQK9-uhf5NFvdwfG7K1xNcCKC4dAakqQ&_hsmi=80362163, accessed 12 June 2020.

344 The complete text of the pledge is available at https://rcrcconference.org/pledge/strengthening-the-resilience-of-communities-to-climate-change-and-environmental-degradation-through-climate-smart-humanitarian-action-renforcer-la-resilience-des-communautes-face-aux-changements-cli/, accessed 12 June 2020.

345 Tignino, *L'eau et la guerre*, *supra* note 1, 414–416.

346 See K. Eklöw & F. Krampe, *Climate-related Security Risks and Peacebuilding in Somalia*, SIPRI Policy Paper 53 (Solna: Stockholm International Peace Research Institute, 2019), at 4; J. Mazo, '*Darfur: The First Modern Climate-Change Conflict*', 49:409, The Adelphi Papers (2009) 73–86.

due to the several years-long drought caused by climate change.[347] Given the increasingly visible impacts of climate change and water stress, issues relating to protection of water infrastructure in armed conflicts will likely have to be prioritized in the future.

Another phenomenon occupying the agendas of law and policy-makers is cyber warfare. As technology develops at much higher speeds than the law, the issue—how are or should cyber warfare be regulated—is surrounded by controversies; here the authors will confine themselves to stating that the existing rules of international humanitarian law continue to apply to all situations of armed conflict. However, water and water-related infrastructure are increasingly dependent on computer networks, and are thus increasingly vulnerable to ever frequent cyber attacks. This issue requires collaboration of different actors and their coordinated action to protect water infrastructure.[348]

3.2 *Next Steps*

In the long term, among the possible ways to ensure the implementation of the principles on the protection of water infrastructure, establishing a mechanism or using an existing institutional mechanism can be considered. The 'zero draft' of the Geneva List included a principle entitled 'Mechanism', which recommended that states strengthen their cooperation on the protection of water infrastructure during and after armed conflict through such a mechanism. This was in pursuance of the recommendation of the Global High-Level Panel on Water and Peace that further consideration be given to establish

> [a]n independent international body mandated to gather information about the destruction and cuts to water supplies as well as to foster technical assistance during protracted armed conflicts; A mechanism to monitor compliance with IHL and reparations to victims of violations; Improved cooperation among the relevant international organizations and agencies to manage post-conflict environmental assessments and

347 P. H. Gleick, '*Water, Drought, Climate Change, and Conflict in Syria*', 6:3, Weather, Climate, and Society (2014) 331–340.

348 See in general on industrial cyber attacks, S. Caltagirone, '*Industrial cyber attacks: A humanitarian crisis in the making*', Humanitarian Law and Policy (3 December 2019), https://blogs.icrc.org/law-and-policy/2019/12/03/industrial-cyber-attacks-crisis/?utm_campaign=DP_Forum%20-%20Industrial%20cyber%20attacks%3A%20a%20humanitarian%20crisis%20in%20the%20making&utm_source=hs_email&utm_medium=email&utm_content=80231354&_hsenc=p2ANqtz-JgRKuPED-p9GU8Px-U4P6QZtxO7KoePIJrcZr5Iki_Q6FLjO9Oljr-y_jOZEhyHJzi2LSkT6qI7uONL6nDYPe4Q13Ew&_hsmi=80231354, accessed 12 June 2020.

> remedial measures; A rapid reaction water engineering military capacity to restore basic water and sanitation services for civilian populations and, in particular, for sensitive sites such as hospitals and refugee camps.[349]

The suggested functions of the mechanism were the collection of hydrological, technical and geographical data; the monitoring of violations of the rules regulating the protection of water infrastructure; serving as a focal point for the coordination of relief activities relating to the reparation of water infrastructure and for fostering exchanges and partnerships between different stakeholders; and organization of assessment missions to document the damage inflicted to water infrastructure following the end of armed conflicts.[350]

In terms of data collection, several UN agencies have programmes or projects specifically on water-data collection and water management. Some examples are the World Meteorological Organization's Global Hydrological Status, the Outlook System (HydroSOS),[351] the Global Hydrometry Support Facility (HydroHub),[352] UNESCO's Water Information Network System (IHP-WINS),[353] the World Water Assessment Programme (WWAP),[354] UNEP's Transboundary Water Assessment Programme (TWAP).[355] In addition, some joint mechanisms established by co-riparian states have collective databases.[356] However, there is still a gap in collecting data on damage to water infrastructure

349 GHLPWP Report, *supra* note 15, at 31.

350 For an example of a cultural damage assessment, see UNESCO, *The Emergency Safeguarding of the Syrian Cultural Heritage Project*, https://en.unesco.org/syrian-observatory/emergency-safeguarding-syrian-cultural-heritage-project, accessed 12 June 2020.

351 World Meteorological Organization (WMO), *HydroSOS*, https://public.wmo.int/en/our-mandate/what-we-do/application-services/hydrosos, accessed 12 June 2020.

352 WMO, *HydroHub, the Global Hydrometry Support Facility of WMO*, https://public.wmo.int/en/projects/hydrohub, accessed 12 June 2020. The hub has been established to 'build operational systems and capacity in hydrometry and water monitoring; expand the base of hydrological data and exchange capabilities; and facilitate free and open data sharing'.

353 UNESCO, *The Water Information Network System (IHP-WINS)*, https://en.unesco.org/ihp-wins, accessed 12 June 2020.

354 UNESCO, *World Water Assessment Programme (UNESCO WWAP)*, http://www.unesco.org/new/en/natural-sciences/environment/water/wwap/about/, accessed 12 June 2020.

355 See Transboundary Waters Assessment Programme (TWAP) website at http://www.geftwap.org, accessed 12 June 2020.

356 See, for example, the Niger Basin Observatory established by the Niger Basin Authority. See Niger Basin Authority, *Niger Basin Observatory*, http://www.abn.ne/index.php?option=com_content&view=article&id.=51%3Alobservatoire-du-bassin-du-niger&catid=47%3Astructures-du-seabn&Itemid=17&lang=en, accessed 12 June 2020. See also Sahara and Sahel Observatory, *North Western Sahara Aquifer System (SASS)*, http://www.oss-online.org/en/north-western-sahara-aquifer-system-sass, accessed 12 June 2020.

and the effects of such damage.[357] In a press release dated 23 March 2020, on World Meteorological Day, the World Meteorological Organization affirmed this gap and emphasized the need to collect internationally coordinated data on water.[358]

In terms of monitoring compliance with law, at least with international humanitarian law by the parties to armed conflicts, there are a couple of mechanisms provided by the Geneva Conventions and their Additional Protocols. These mechanisms are the Protecting Powers,[359] the enquiry mechanism[360] and the International Humanitarian Fact-Finding Commission.[361] However, these mechanisms are virtually never used. Within the UN system, the UN Security Council established the Monitoring and Reporting Mechanism in 2005, tasked with collecting and providing information on violations and abuses committed against children affected by armed conflict,[362] which include attacks against schools and hospitals and the denial of humanitarian access for children as 'grave violations'.[363] Lastly, in post-conflict situations, UNEP has been carrying out post-conflict environmental assessments since 1999, demonstrating the magnitude of the impacts that conflicts have on

357 See, for example, the Third Report of Jacobsson, *supra* note 290, para 146: 'In the case before the International Court of Justice between Uganda and the Democratic Republic of the Congo, one of the challenges related to the lack of data necessary to prove environmental harm and damage caused in connection to a violation of the prohibition against attacking installations containing dangerous forces. Such a lack of information was also mentioned in the final report to the Prosecutor of the International Tribunal for the Former Yugoslavia by the committee established to review the NATO military operations during the Balkan wars. Efforts to gather reliable information would be more manageable if the information was less fragmented and could be collected in a more systematic fashion. Improving the expediency of justice would benefit both the claimant and defendant in such cases' (footnotes omitted).

358 WMO, 'World Meteorological Day focus on Climate Change and Water', Press Release (23 March 2020).

359 Articles 8/8/8/9 respectively of the four Geneva Conventions of 1949, *supra* note 35; Additional Protocol I, *supra* note 35, Art. 5.

360 Articles 52/53/132/149 respectively of the four Geneva Conventions of 1949, *supra* note 35.

361 Additional Protocol I, *supra* note 35, Art. 90.

362 United Nations Security Council, '*Children and armed conflict*', 26 July 2005, UNSC Resolution 1612, UN Doc. S/RES/1612, para 2(a).

363 UN Office of the Special Representative of the Secretary-General for Children and Armed Conflict, *Monitoring and Reporting on Grave Violations*, https://childrenandarmedconflict.un.org/tools-for-action/monitoring-and-reporting/, accessed 12 June 2020. UNICEF co-chairs the Country Task Force on Monitoring and Reporting in all countries on the agenda of the Office of the Special Representative of the Secretary-General for Children and Armed Conflict.

natural resources, including water.[364] These mechanisms can be explored to see whether they can be employed for enhancing protection of water and water infrastructure, and all can serve as examples during a future discussion on a new mechanism devoted to their protection.

In the short term, the Geneva List project will continue to be carried out with different activities aimed at better understanding the violations of the rules on the protection of water infrastructure and the ways to enhance compliance therewith. Under the auspices of the GWH, the Geneva List will be followed by a series of reports. One report will be devoted to the current status of the implementation of the international law rules governing the protection of water infrastructure in domestic frameworks, such as legislation, directives and military manuals. Another will focus on accountability and analyse the existing jurisprudence, even if limited, both on state responsibility and individual criminal responsibility relating to water and water infrastructure. Regarding state responsibility, human rights mechanisms could be used to enhance the protection of water and water infrastructure, especially through the enforcement of the right to water. For example, in a 2010 decision, the African Commission on Human and People's Rights ruled against the Sudanese government for the violation of the right to water during the conflict in Darfur and ordered the rehabilitation of water infrastructure to allow and facilitate the return of displaced persons.[365] In respect of international criminal law, the main rules of international law that directly and indirectly criminalize acts harmful to water infrastructure have been illustrated in Principle 24. However, here a development which took place after the finalization of the Geneva List in August 2019 should be noted. Following a Swiss proposal, the ICC Assembly of States Parties took a unanimous decision to make starvation punishable when committed in non-international conflicts.[366] As starvation also comprises deprivation of water, this progress will contribute to the enrichment of the international jurisprudence on water-related crimes.

Compliance with the rules on the protection of water infrastructure may be ensured through several means, including by training armed forces, assessing and reporting the damage to water infrastructure, and holding responsible those who have committed war crimes relating to water. Acceptance of the

---

364 UNEP, *Post-Conflict Environmental Assessment*, https://www.unenvironment.org/explore-topics/disasters-conflicts/where-we-work/cote-divoire/post-conflict-environmental, accessed 12 June 2020.

365 *Centre of Housing Rights and Evictions v. The Sudan*, *supra* note 293, paras 228, 229(5).

366 Switzerland, *supra* note 334.

recommendations that go beyond existing law may be enabled through persistent advocacy and awareness raising by academics and practitioners. The development of hydro-diplomacy among states may also contribute to the implementation of the recommendations enshrined in the Geneva List.

Annex: The Geneva List of Principles on the Protection of Water Infrastructure

Principle 1: Objective and Scope

1. The objective of the Geneva List is to ensure the protection of water infrastructure and water-related infrastructure during armed conflicts as well as to safeguard their utilization in post-conflict situations.
2. The Geneva List is intended for international and non-international armed conflicts as well as post-conflict situations.
3. The Geneva List is addressed to States and non-State actors.
4. The Geneva List is without prejudice to the applicable obligations of States and non-State actors under international law.

Principle 2: Definitions

For the purposes of the Geneva List:

(a) 'Water infrastructure' means all water and wastewater works, installations and facilities;

(b) 'Water-related infrastructure' means facilities, installations and other works which make an essential contribution to the functioning of water infrastructure so that their destruction or damage would render the water infrastructure inoperable.

Principle 3: The Human Rights to Water and Sanitation

Everyone has the rights to water and sanitation, which are essential for the full enjoyment of all human rights.

Principle 4: Use of Water Infrastructure and Water-Related Infrastructure as a Means of Warfare

1. The parties to the conflict should refrain from using water infrastructure and water-related infrastructure as a means of warfare.
2. In cases where water infrastructure and water-related infrastructure are used as a means of warfare during the conduct of hostilities, the principles of distinction, proportionality and precautions must be respected.

Principle 5: Poison or Poisoned Weapons

The use of poison or poisoned weapons against water and water infrastructure is prohibited.

Principle 6: Attacks against Water Infrastructure and Water-Related Infrastructure

Water infrastructure and water-related infrastructure are presumed to be civilian objects and, in such case, must not be attacked.

Principle 7: Attacks against the Personnel Working for Water Infrastructure and Water-Related Infrastructure

Personnel responsible for carrying out tasks related to the operation, maintenance, assessment, repair and rehabilitation of water infrastructure and water-related infrastructure are presumed to be civilians and, in such case, must not be attacked.

Principle 8: Indiscriminate Attacks

Attacks which do not or cannot distinguish between military objectives and civilian objects, including water infrastructure and water-related infrastructure, are prohibited.

Principle 9: Proportionality in Attack

1. Attacks against water infrastructure and water-related infrastructure, when these are military objectives, which may be expected to cause incidental loss of civilian life, injury to civilians, damage to civilian objects, or a combination thereof, which would be excessive in relation to the concrete and direct military advantage anticipated, are prohibited.
2. Attacks against military objectives which may be expected to cause incidental loss of civilian life, injury to civilians, damage to civilian objects, including water infrastructure and water-related infrastructure, or a combination thereof, which would be excessive in relation to the concrete and direct military advantage anticipated, are prohibited.
3. The reverberating, or indirect, effects that are foreseeable in the circumstances at the time of the attack should be taken into account in the assessment of proportionality.

Principle 10: Precautions in Attack

1. In the conduct of military operations, constant care must be taken to spare the civilian population, civilians and civilian objects, including water infrastructure and water-related infrastructure.

2. Prior to an attack against water infrastructure or water-related infrastructure, those who plan, decide upon and execute attacks must do everything feasible to verify that these are military objectives and that it is not prohibited to attack them.
3. Those who plan, decide upon and execute attacks, including against water infrastructure and water-related infrastructure, must take all feasible precautions with a view to avoiding, and in any event to minimizing, incidental loss of civilian life, injury to civilians and damage to civilian objects, including water infrastructure and water-related infrastructure.

Principle 11: Precautions against the Effects of Attacks

1. The parties to the conflict must take all feasible precautions to protect the civilian population and civilian objects, including water infrastructure and water-related infrastructure, under their control against the effects of attacks.
2. The parties to the conflict should avoid locating military objectives in the vicinity of water infrastructure and water-related infrastructure.
3. The parties to the conflict are encouraged to establish protected zones around water infrastructure and water-related infrastructure.

Principle 12: Starvation and Water Infrastructure Indispensable to the Survival of the Civilian Population

1. The use of starvation of the civilian population as a method of warfare is prohibited.
2. The parties to the conflict must not attack, destroy, remove or render useless water infrastructure indispensable to the survival of the civilian population.

Principle 13: Water Infrastructure Containing Dangerous Forces

1. Water infrastructure containing dangerous forces, namely dams and dykes, even when these are military objectives, and other military objectives located at or in their vicinity, should not be made the object of attack, if such attack may cause the release of dangerous forces and consequent severe losses among the civilian population.
2. In any case, particular care must be taken if dams, dykes and other installations located at or in their vicinity are attacked, in order to avoid release of dangerous forces and consequent severe losses among the civilian population.

3. The parties to the conflict are encouraged to extend the protection provided for dams and dykes to all water infrastructure containing dangerous forces.

Principle 14: Acts or Threats of Violence the Primary Purpose of Which Is to Spread Terror among the Civilian Population

Acts or threats of violence the primary purpose of which is to spread terror among the civilian population, including but not limited to the release of dangerous forces from dams and dykes, and the poisoning or retention of water, are prohibited.

Principle 15: Protection of the Environment

Water infrastructure and water-related infrastructure should not be made the object of attack, even when these are military objectives, if such attack is intended, or may be expected, to cause significant damage to the environment.

Principle 16: Forced Displacement

The control over the delivery of water, and deprivation thereof, must not be used to force the displacement of civilians.

Principle 17: Humanitarian Access and Assistance

1. Humanitarian relief personnel, including those involved in water-related activities, and their equipment must be respected and protected.
2. The parties to the conflict must allow and facilitate rapid and unimpeded passage of humanitarian relief personnel, including those involved in water-related activities, and their equipment for the operation, maintenance, assessment, repair and rehabilitation of water infrastructure and water-related infrastructure, especially those which provide water indispensable to the survival of the civilian population.
3. Civil defence organizations, including those involved in the repair and rehabilitation of water infrastructure and water-related infrastructure, and their personnel must be respected and protected.
4. The parties to the conflict are encouraged to negotiate water ceasefire agreements in order to allow the safe passage of humanitarian relief personnel, including those involved in water-related activities.
5. The parties to the conflict are encouraged to collaborate for the operation, maintenance, assessment, repair and rehabilitation of water infrastructure and water-related infrastructure.

Principle 18: Occupation

The Occupying Power must restore and ensure public order and civil life in the occupied territory, including through the maintenance of water infrastructure and water-related infrastructure essential for the provision of water and sanitation services.

Principle 19: Peace Agreements

1. Peace agreements must not deprive peoples of their rights to water and sanitation.
2. Peace agreements should be concluded in accordance with the principle of equitable and reasonable utilization of water resources.

Principle 20: Joint Mechanisms and Commissions

Watercourse States should create joint mechanisms and commissions, or in any case cooperate and coordinate, with a view to ensuring the protection, safe operation and maintenance of water infrastructure located on transboundary water resources.

Principle 21: Reconstruction, Rehabilitation and Repair of Water Infrastructure and Water-Related Infrastructure

1. Destroyed and damaged water infrastructure and water-related infrastructure should be reconstructed, rehabilitated and repaired.
2. The equipment and other goods necessary for the reconstruction, rehabilitation, repair, operation and maintenance of water infrastructure and water-related infrastructure should be exempted from sanctions and other coercive measures.

Principle 22: Peacekeeping Operations

1. Protection of water infrastructure and water-related infrastructure and their reconstruction, rehabilitation and repair should be included in the mandates of the peacekeeping operations, where appropriate.
2. Peacekeeping operations should support and provide assistance to the local authorities in the reconstruction, rehabilitation, repair, operation and maintenance of the water infrastructure and water-related infrastructure.

Principle 23: Martens Clause

In cases not covered by international agreements, water infrastructure and water-related infrastructure remain under the protection and authority of the principles of international law derived from established custom, the principles of humanity and the dictates of public conscience.

Principle 24: Implementation

1. States must incorporate in their domestic frameworks their obligations relating to the protection of water infrastructure stemming from international law, as applicable.
2. States must implement in their domestic frameworks international crimes relating to the protection of water infrastructure, as applicable.
3. States are encouraged to incorporate in their domestic frameworks the recommendations of the Geneva List.

Author Biographies

Mara Tignino is a Reader at the Faculty of Law and the Institute for Environmental Sciences of the University of Geneva and the Lead Legal Specialist of the Platform for International Water Law of the Geneva Water Hub. Dr Tignino has been Visiting Professor at Renmin University of China, the University of Barcelona, the LUISS of Rome, and the Catholic University of Lille. She was also a Visiting Scholar at the George Washington University Law School in Washington D.C. She acts as an expert and legal adviser for States and international organisations. She holds a *Diplôme d'études supérieures* and a Ph.D. in international law from the Graduate Institute of International and Development Studies in Geneva. She received her *Habilitation à diriger des recherches* (*HDR*) from the Faculty of Law of the University Jean Moulin Lyon 3. She received her Bachelor's degree in Political Science from the LUISS and a *Certificat d'études politiques européennes* from the *Institut d'Études Politiques* of Strasbourg.

Öykü Irmakkesen is a PhD candidate at the University of Geneva and a Teaching Assistant at the Geneva Academy of International Humanitarian Law and Human Rights. She previously worked as a Researcher at the Geneva Water Hub's Platform for International Water Law and as a Legal Associate at the International Committee of the Red Cross. She has also worked as an Assistant Programme Coordinator for the Syrians' Protection Programme at the Association for Solidarity with Asylum Seekers and Migrants (Turkey). She holds an LLM in International Humanitarian Law and Human Rights from the Geneva Academy.

Bibliography

Agreement on the Cooperation for the Sustainable Development of the Mekong River Basin (5 April 1995).

Amnesty International, *Dead Land: Islamic State's Deliberate Destruction of Iraq's Farmland* (London: Amnesty International, 2018).

Amnesty International, *Troubled Waters: Palestinians Denied Fair Access to Water: Israel-Occupied Palestinian Territories* (London: Amnesty International, 2009).

Australia, *Law of Armed Conflict*, Australian Defence Doctrine Publication 06.4 (11 May 2006).

Bothe, M., K. J. Partsch & W. A. Solf, *New Rules for Victims of Armed Conflicts: Commentary on the Two 1977 Protocols Additional to the Geneva Conventions 1949* (2nd edition, Leiden: Martinus Nijhoff Publishers, 2013).

Boutruche, T., '*Le statut de l'eau en droit international humanitaire*', 82:240, International Review of the Red Cross (2000) 887–916.

Bryne Nason, Ambassador Geraldine, 'Joint Statement on Explosive Weapons in Populated Areas', 73rd session of the UN General Assembly (25 October 2018).

Caltagirone, S., '*Industrial cyber attacks: A humanitarian crisis in the making*', Humanitarian Law and Policy (3 December 2019).

Canada, *Use of Force for CF Operations*, Canadian Forces Joint Publication, B-GJ-005-501/FP-001 (August 2008).

Centre of Housing Rights and Evictions v. The Sudan, African Commission on Human and People's Rights, 279/03-296/05 (2009).

Charter of Waters of the River Senegal (28 May 2002).

Clapham, A., '*Focusing on armed non-state actors*', in A. Clapham & P. Gaeta, (eds.), *The Oxford Handbook of International Law in Armed Conflict* (Oxford: Oxford University Press, 2014) 766–810.

Clapham, A., '*Non-state actors*', in D. Moeckli, S. Shah & S. Sivakumaran, (eds.), *International Human Rights Law* (3rd edition, Oxford: Oxford University Press, 2018) 557–579.

Čolakhodžić, A., M. Filipović, J. Kovandžić & S. Stephen, '*The Sava River: Transitioning to peace in the former Yugoslavia*' in E. Weinthal, J. Troell, & M. Nakayaman, (eds.), *Water and Post-Conflict Peacebuilding* (London: Earthscan, 2013).

Convention on Cluster Munitions (30 May 2008).

Convention on Cooperation for the Protection and Sustainable Use of the Danube River (29 June 1994).

Convention on Environmental Impact Assessment in a Transboundary Context (25 February 1991).

Convention on the Elimination of All Forms of Discrimination Against Women (18 December 1979).

Convention on the Law of Non-navigational Uses of International Watercourses (21 May 1997).

Convention on the Prohibition of Military or Any Other Hostile Use of Environmental Modification Techniques (10 December 1976).

Convention on the Prohibition of the Use, Stockpiling, Production and Transfer of Anti-Personnel Mines (18 September 1997).

Convention on the Protection of Transboundary Watercourses and International Lakes (17 March 1992).

Convention on the Rights of Persons with Disabilities (13 December 2006).

Convention on the Rights of the Child (20 November 1989).

Damluji, N., '*Legal Analysis: Daesh Control of Watercourses in Syria and in Iraq*', 25, Pacific Rim Law and Policy Journal (2106) 331–363.

Darfur Peace Agreement (5 May 2006).

Declaration Renouncing the Use, in Time of War, of Explosive Projectiles Under 400 Grammes Weight (11 December 1868).

Droege, C., & M.-L. Tougas, '*The Protection of the Natural Environment in Armed Conflict: Existing Rules and Need for Further Legal Protection*', 82, Nordic Journal of International Law (2013) 21–52.

Eklöw, K., & F. Krampe, *Climate-related Security Risks and Peacebuilding in Somalia*, SIPRI Policy Paper 53 (Solna: Stockholm International Peace Research Institute, 2019).

European Union, Delegation to Georgia, 'EU Assistance to People Affected by Conflict in Georgia', Overview (2011).

Ferraro, T., (ed.), *Occupation and Other Forms of Administration of Foreign Territory* (*Expert Meeting Report*) (Geneva: International Committee of the Red Cross, 2012).

Final Act of the Vienna Congress (9 June 1815).

Final Agreement to End the Armed Conflict and Build a Stable and Lasting Peace (24 November 2016) between the National Government of Colombia and the Revolutionary Armed Forces of Colombia—People's Army (FARC-EP).

Food and Agriculture Organization of the United Nations (FAO), *Systematic Index of International Water Resources Treaties, Declarations, Acts and Cases by Basin*, Legislative Study No. 15 (Rome: FAO, 1978).

Fortin, K., *The Accountability of Armed Groups under Human Rights Law* (Oxford: Oxford University Press, 2017).

Framework Agreement on the Sava River Basin (3 December 2002).

France, *Fiche de Synthèse sur les Règles Applicables dans les Conflits Armés*, Note No. 432/DEF/EMA/OL.2/NP (1992).

France, *Manuel de droit des conflits armés* (Ministère de la Défense, 2001).
General Act of the Berlin Conference (26 February 1885).
Geneva Convention for the Amelioration of the Condition of the Wounded and Sick in Armed Forces in the Field (12 August 1949).
Geneva Convention for the Amelioration of the Condition of Wounded, Sick and Shipwrecked Members of Armed Forces at Sea (12 August 1949).
Geneva Convention relative to the Protection of Civilian Persons in Time of War (12 August 1949).
Geneva Convention relative to the Treatment of Prisoners of War (12 August 1949).
Geneva Water Hub, *Determined Steps* (2019).
Geneva Water Hub, *Protection of Water During and After Armed Conflicts* (2016).
Germany, *Humanitarian Law in Armed Conflicts—Manual*, DSK VV207320067, The Federal Ministry of Defence of the Federal Republic of Germany, VR II 3 (August 1992), English translation of ZDv 15/2.
Gillard, E.-C., *'Proportionality in the Conduct of Hostilities: The Incidental Harm Side of the Assessment'*, Research Paper (London: Chatham House, 2018).
Gisel, L., (ed.), *The Principle of Proportionality in the Rules Governing the Conduct of Hostilities under International Humanitarian Law, International Expert Meeting Report, 22–23 June 2016, Quebec* (Geneva: International Committee of the Red Cross, 2018).
Gleick, P. H., *'Water, Drought, Climate Change, and Conflict in Syria'*, 6:3, Weather, Climate, and Society (2014) 331–340.
Global High-Level Panel on Water and Peace, *A Matter of Survival* (*Report*) (Geneva: Geneva Water Hub, 2017).
Grzybowski, A., *Innovations in Trans-boundary Water Management: Pacific Resolutions* (United Nations Regional Centre for Preventive Diplomacy for Central Asia, 2013).
Hague Convention (II) with respect to the Laws and Customs of War on Land and its Annex: Regulations concerning the Laws and Customs of War on Land (29 July 1899).
Hague Convention (IV) Respecting the Laws and Customs of War on Land and its Annex: Regulations concerning the Laws and Customs of War on Land (18 October 1907).
Henckaerts, J.-M., & L. Doswald-Beck (eds.), *Customary International Humanitarian Law* (Cambridge and Geneva: Cambridge University Press and International Committee of the Red Cross, 2005).
High-Level Panel on Water, *Making Every Drop Count: An Agenda for Water Action* (*Outcome Document*) (United Nations Department of Economic and Social Affairs/World Bank, 2018).
Human Rights Watch, *Turkey/Syria: Weaponizing Water in Global Pandemic?*, 31 March 2020.
Humanitarian Ceasefire Agreement on the Conflict in Darfur (8 April 2004).

IHL in action, *Iraq, Computer Modelling in Collateral Damage Estimates and Choice of Weapons* (International Committee of the Red Cross, n.d.).

Indus Waters Treaty (16 September 1960).

Instructions for the Government of Armies of the United States in the Field (Lieber Code) (24 April 1863).

International Committee of the Red Cross, *Bled Dry: How War in the Middle East is Bringing the Region's Water Supplies to Breaking Point* (Geneva: ICRC, 2015).

International Committee of the Red Cross, '*Civil Defence in International Humanitarian Law*', Factsheet (2001).

International Committee of the Red Cross, '*Explosive Weapons in Populated Areas*', Factsheet (2016).

International Committee of the Red Cross, '*Guidelines for Military Manuals and Instructions on the Protection of the Environment in Times of Armed Conflict*', 311, International Review of the Red Cross (30 April 1994).

International Committee of the Red Cross, *International Humanitarian Law and the Challenges of Contemporary Armed Conflicts Report*, Doc 32IC/15/11 (October 2015).

International Committee of the Red Cross, 'Protection of the civilian population in period of armed conflict', Resolution 2, 26th International Conference (7 December 1995).

International Committee of the Red Cross, *Syria: Water Used as Weapon of War*, News Release (2 September 2015).

International Committee of the Red Cross, *Urban Services during Protracted Armed Conflicts: A Call for a Better Approach to Assisting Affected People* (Geneva: International Committee of the Red Cross, 2015).

International Committee of the Red Cross, *Water and War: ICRC Response* (Geneva: ICRC, 2009).

International Court of Justice, Case concerning Armed Activities on the Territory of the Congo (Democratic Republic of the Congo v. Uganda), Judgment, 19 December 2005.

International Court of Justice, Case concerning Pulp Mills on the River Uruguay (Argentina v. Uruguay), Judgment, 20 April 2010.

International Court of Justice, Case Concerning the Gabčíkovo-Nagymaros Project (Hungary v. Slovakia), Judgment, 25 September 1997.

International Court of Justice, Legal Consequences of the Construction of a Wall in the Occupied Palestinian Territory, Advisory Opinion, 9 July 2004.

International Court of Justice, Legality of the Threat or Use of Nuclear Weapons, Advisory Opinion, 8 July 1996.

International Court of Justice, Legality of the Threat or Use of Nuclear Weapons (Advisory Opinion), Written statement of the Marshall Islands (22 June 1995).

International Court of Justice, Legality of the Threat or Use of Nuclear Weapons (Advisory Opinion), Written statement of Sweden (20 June 1995).

International Court of Justice, Legality of the Threat or Use of Nuclear Weapons (Advisory Opinion), Written statement of the United Kingdom (16 June 1995).

International Court of Justice, Legality of the Threat or Use of Nuclear Weapons (Advisory Opinion), Written statement of the United States of America (20 June 1995).

International Covenant on Civil and Political Rights (16 December 1966).

International Covenant on Economic, Social and Cultural Rights (16 December 1966).

International Criminal Court, Office of the Prosecutor, 'Annex A to the Public Redacted Version of the Prosecutor's Application under Article 58 (Situation in Darfur, the Sudan)' (2008).

International Criminal Tribunal for the Former Yugoslavia, *Final Report to the Prosecutor by the Committee Established to Review the NATO Bombing Campaign Against the Federal Republic of Yugoslavia* (13 June 2000).

International Institute of Humanitarian Law (L. Doswald-Beck, ed.), *San Remo Manual on International Law Applicable to Armed Conflicts at Sea* (Cambridge and New York: Cambridge University Press, 1995).

International Law Association, '*International Water Resources Law*', Report of the Fifty-seventh Conference, Madrid, 30 August–4 September 1976 (London, 1978) 213–266.

International Law Association, '*Resolution on the Protection of Water Resources and Water Installations in Times of Armed Conflict*', Report of the Fifty-seventh Conference, Madrid, 30 August–4 September 1976 (London, 1978) 237–239.

International Law Association, '*The Berlin Rules on Water Resources*', Report of the Seventy-first Conference, Berlin, 16–21 August 2004 (London, 2004) 337–411.

International Law Commission, '*Draft Articles on Prevention of Transboundary Harm from Hazardous Activities*', II:Part II, Yearbook of the International Law Commission (2001) 148–170.

International Law Commission, '*Draft Articles on the Law of the Non-navigational Uses of International Watercourses and Commentaries Thereto and Resolution on Transboundary Confined Groundwater*', II:Part II, Yearbook of the International Law Commission (1994) 89–135.

International Law Commission, '*Draft Articles on the Law of Transboundary Aquifers, with commentaries*', II:Part II Yearbook of the International Law Commission (2008) 19–43.

International Law Commission, '*Draft Principles on the Allocation of Loss in the Case of Transboundary Harm Arising Out of Hazardous Activities*', II:Part II, Yearbook of the International Law Commission (2006) 59–90.

International Law Commission, *Protection of the Environment in Relation to Armed Conflict*, Doc A/CN.4/L.937 (6 June 2019).

International Law Commission, *Second Report on Protection of the Environment in relation to armed conflicts by Marja Lehto, Special Rapporteur*, Doc A/CN.4/728 (27 March 2019).

International Law Commission, *Third Report on the Law of the Non-navigational Uses of International Watercourses, by Mr. Stephen M. Schwebel, Special Rapporteur*, Doc A/CN.4/348 (11 December 1981).

International Law Commission, *Third Report on the Protection of the Environment in Relation to Armed Conflicts submitted by Marie G. Jacobsson, Special Rapporteur*, Doc A/CN.4/700 (3 June 2016).

Israel, 'Gaza Operation Investigations: Second Update', Ministry of Foreign Affairs of Israel (July 2010).

Israel Ministry of Foreign Affairs, 'Preserving Humanitarian Principles While Combating Terrorism: Israel's Struggle with Hezbollah in the Lebanon War', Diplomatic Notes No. 1, (April 2007).

Jorgensen, N., '*The Protection of Freshwater in Armed Conflict*', 3:2, Journal of International Law and International Relations (2007) 57–96.

Lindsey-Curtet, C., F. Tercier Holst-Roness & L. Anderson, *Addressing the Needs of Women Affected by Armed Conflict: An ICRC Guidance Document* (Geneva: International Committee of the Red Cross, 2004).

Lune-Grayson, C., '*When Rain Turns to Dust: Climate Change, Conflict and Humanitarian Action*', Humanitarian Law and Policy (5 December 2019).

Macharis, O., & N. Farajalla, *Case Study on the 2006 Israel-Lebanon War and its Impact on Water Resources and Water Infrastructure in Lebanon* (on file with the authors).

Mazo, J., '*Darfur: The First Modern Climate-Change Conflict*', 49:409, The Adelphi Papers (2009) 73–86.

Melzer, N., *Interpretive Guidance on the Notion of Direct Participation in Hostilities under International Humanitarian Law* (Geneva: International Committee of the Red Cross, 2009).

Nuremberg International Military Tribunal, *Trial of the Major War Criminals, 14 November 1945–1 October 1946*, Nuremberg, 1947, Vol. 1.

Official Records of the Diplomatic Conference on the Reaffirmation and Development of International Humanitarian Law Applicable in Armed Conflicts (Geneva, 1974–1977) (Federal Political Department, Bern 1978), Vol. XV, CDDH/III/264/Rev.1.

Organization for Security and Co-operation in Europe, Mission to Georgia, *Economic Rehabilitation Works*, Issue 1 (Tbilisi: OSCE, 2008).

Organization for Security and Co-operation in Europe, Special Monitoring Mission to Ukraine, *Access to Water in Conflict-affected Areas of Donetsk and Luhansk Regions* (Vienna: OSCE, 2015).

Parliamentary Assembly of the Council of Europe, *Economic Reconstruction and Renewal in South-eastern Europe Following the Kosovo Conflict, Addendum to the Report*, Doc 8503, (16 September 1999).

Permanent Court of Arbitration, *Indus Water Kishenganga Arbitration* (*Islamic Republic of Pakistan v. Republic of India*), Final Award, 20 December 2013.

Program on Humanitarian Policy and Conflict Research at Harvard University, *HPCR Manual on International Law Applicable to Air and Missile Warfare* (New York: Cambridge University Press, 2013).

Prosecutor v. Stanislav Galić, Judgment, Trial Chamber, IT-98-29-T (5 December 2003).

Protocol Additional to the Geneva Conventions of 12 August 1949, and relating to the Protection of Victims of International Armed Conflicts (8 June 1977).

Protocol Additional to the Geneva Conventions of 12 August 1949, and relating to the Protection of Victims of Non-International Armed Conflicts (8 June 1977).

Protocol on Prohibitions or Restrictions on the Use of Mines, Booby-Traps and other Devices as amended on 3 May 1996, annexed to the Convention on Prohibitions or Restrictions on the Use of Certain Conventional Weapons Which May Be Deemed to Be Excessively Injurious or to Have Indiscriminate Effects (3 May 1996).

Remans, W., '*Water and War*', 8:1, Humantäres Völkerrecht (1995) 1–14.

Revised Protocol on Shared Watercourses in the Southern African Development Community (7 August 2000).

Rome Statute of the International Criminal Court (17 July 1998).

Sandoz, Y., C. Swinarski & B. Zimmerman, *Commentary on the Additional Protocols of 8 June 1977 to the Geneva Conventions of 12 August 1949* (Geneva: International Committee of the Red Cross and Martinus Nijhoff Publishers, 1987).

Sands, P., & J. Peel, *Principles of International Environmental Law* (4th edition, Cambridge: Cambridge University Press, 2018).

Sangbana, K., '*The Role of Non-State Actors in the Development and Implementation of International Water Law*' in A. Rieu-Clarke, A. Allan & S. Hendry, *Routledge Handbook of Water Law and Policy* (London: Routledge, 2017) 287–296.

Sassòli, M., A. Bouvier & A. Quintin (eds.), 'Martens Clause', *How Does Law Protect in War?, Online Casebook 2.0* (ICRC, 2014).

Schmitt, M. N., (ed.), *Tallinn Manual 2.0 on the International Law Applicable to Cyber Operations* (Cambridge: Cambridge University Press, 2017).

Sowers, J. L., E. Weinthal & N. Zawahri, '*Targeting Environmental Infrastructures, International Law, and Civilians in the New Middle Eastern Wars*', 48:5, Security Dialogue (2017) 410–430.

Stucki, P., *Water Wars or Water Peace? Rethinking the Nexus between Water Scarcity and Armed Conflict*, Programme for Strategic and International Security Studies, Occasional Paper No. 3 (Geneva: Graduate Institute of International and Development Studies, 2005).

Tignino, M., *L'eau et la guerre. Eléments pour un régime juridique* (Brussels: Bruylant, 2011).

Tignino, M., '*Water During and After Armed Conflicts: What Protection in International Law?*', 1:4 Brill Research Perspectives in International Water Law (2016).

Treaty of Paris (30 March 1856).
Treaty of Peace between The Hashemite Kingdom of Jordan and The State of Israel (26 October 1994).
Treaty of Peace with Turkey (24 July 1923).
Treaty of Versailles (28 June 1919).
United Kingdom, *The Law of War on Land being Part III of the Manual of Military Law* (The War Office, 1958).
United Kingdom, *The Manual of the Law of Armed Conflict* (Ministry of Defence, 1 July 2004).
United Nations, *Conflict-related Sexual Violence: Report of the Secretary-General*, UN Doc S/2019/280 (29 March 2019).
United Nations Children's Fund, 'Eight Water Facilities Come Under Attack in Idlib, Northwest of Syria, Affecting Water Supply for Nearly 250,000 People', Statement (20 July 2019).
United Nations Children's Fund, 'Interruption to Key Water Station in the Northeast of Syria Puts 460,000 People at Risk as Efforts Ramp Up to Prevent the Spread of Coronavirus Disease', Statement (23 March 2020).
United Nations Children's Fund, *Protecting Children from Unsafe Water in Gaza: Strategy, Action Plan and Project Resources* (UNICEF, 2011).
United Nations Children's Fund, *Water Under Fire: Emergencies, Development and Peace in Fragile and Conflict-affected Contexts*, Volume 1 (UNICEF, 2019).
United Nations Children's Fund and World Health Organization, *Progress on Household Drinking Water, Sanitation and Hygiene 2000–2017: Special Focus on Inequalities* (New York: UNICEF and WHO, 2019).
United Nations Commission on Human Rights, *Report on the Situation of Human Rights in Kuwait under Iraqi Occupation, prepared by Mr. Walter Kälin, Special Rapporteur of the Commission on Human Rights, in accordance with Commission resolution 1991/74*, Doc E/CN.4/1992/26 (16 January 1992).
United Nations Commission on Human Rights, *The Right to Food, Report submitted by the Special Rapporteur on the Right to food, Jean Ziegler, in accordance with Commission on Human Rights Resolution 2002/25*, Doc E/CN.4/2003/54 (10 January 2003).
United Nations Committee on Economic, Social and Cultural Rights, 'General Comment No. 7: The right to adequate housing (Art. 11(1) of the Covenant): Forced evictions' (1997).
United Nations Committee on Economic, Social and Cultural Rights, 'General Comment No. 8: The relationship between economic sanctions and respect for economic, social and cultural rights' (1997).
United Nations Committee on Economic, Social and Cultural Rights, 'General Comment No. 15: The right to water (Arts. 11 and 12 of the Covenant)' (2003).

United Nations Committee on Economic, Social and Cultural Rights, 'General Comment No. 20: Non-discrimination in economic, social and cultural rights (art. 2, para. 2, of the International Covenant on Economic, Social and Cultural Rights)' (2009).

United Nations Conference on Environment and Development, *Rio Declaration on Environment and Development*, UN Doc A/CONF.151/26 (Vol. 1) (12 August 1992).

United Nations Department of Economic and Social Affairs, *A Gender Perspective on Water Resources and Sanitation*, Background Paper No. 2, UN Doc DESA/DSD/2005/2 (2005).

United Nations Department of Public Information, *UN Peace Operations: Year in Review* (2004).

United Nations Department of Public Information, *UN Peace Operations: Year in Review* (2012).

United Nations Economic and Social Council, *Guiding Principles on Internal Displacement*, UN Doc E/CN.4/1998/53/Add.2 (11 February 1998).

United Nations Environment Programme, *Environmental Assessment of the Gaza Strip following the Escalation of Hostilities in December 2008–January 2009* (Nairobi: UNEP, 2009).

United Nations Environment Programme, *Greening the Blue Helmets: Environment, Natural Resources and UN Peacekeeping Operations* (Nairobi: UNEP, 2012).

United Nations Environment Programme, *Sudan: Post-Conflict Environmental Assessment* (Nairobi: UNEP, 2007).

United Nations Environment Programme and United Nations Centre for Human Settlements, *The Kosovo Conflict: Consequences for the Environment and Human Settlements* (Nairobi: UNEP and UNCHS, 1999).

United Nations Environment Programme and United Nations Country Team in Afghanistan, *Natural Resource Management, and Peacebuilding in Afghanistan* (Nairobi: UNEP, 2013).

United Nations General Assembly, '*The Situation in Bosnia and Herzegovina*', 20 December 1993, UNGA Resolution 48/88, UN Doc. A/RES/48/88.

United Nations General Assembly, '*The human rights to safe drinking water and sanitation*', 17 December 2015, UNGA Resolution 70/169, UN Doc. A/RES/70/169.

United Nations General Assembly, '*The human rights to safe drinking water and sanitation*'. 19 December 2017, UNGA Resolution 72/178, UN Doc. A/RES/72/178.

United Nations General Assembly, *Report of the High-Level Independent Panel on Peace on Uniting our Strengths for Peace: Politics, Partnership and People*, UN Doc A/70/95 (17 June 2015).

United Nations Human Rights Committee, *General Comment No. 27: Freedom of Movement (Article 12)*, UN Doc CCPR/C/21/Rev.1/Add.9 (1 November 1999).

United Nations Human Rights Council, *Report of the Independent International Commission of Inquiry on Syrian Arab Republic*, UN Doc A/HRC/31/68 (11 February 2016).

United Nations Human Rights Council, *Report of the Independent International Commission of Inquiry on the Syrian Arab Republic*, UN Doc A/HRC/34/64 (2 February 2017).

United Nations Human Rights Council, *Report of the Special Rapporteur on the Human Rights to Safe Drinking Water and Sanitation*, UN Doc A/HRC/39/55 (3 August 2018).

United Nations Human Rights Council, *Report of the Special Rapporteur on the Human Rights to Safe Drinking Water and Sanitation, Catarina de Albuquerque, Stigma and the Realization of the Human Rights to Water and Sanitation*, UN Doc A/HRC/21/42 (2 July 2012).

United Nations Human Rights Council, *Report of the Special Rapporteur on the Negative Impact of Unilateral Coercive Measures on the Enjoyment of Human Rights*, UN Doc A/HRC/36/44 (26 July 2017).

United Nations Human Rights Council, *Report of the Special Rapporteur on the Situation of Human Rights in the Palestinian Territories Occupied Since 1967*, UN Doc A/HRC/40/73 (15 March 2019).

United Nations Human Rights Council, *Thematic Study of the Office of the United Nations High Commissioner for Human Rights on the Impact of Unilateral Coercive Measures on the Enjoyment of Human Rights, including Recommendations on Actions Aimed at Ending Such Measures*, UN Doc A/HRC/19/33 (11 January 2012).

United Nations Human Rights Council, '*Human rights and access to safe drinking water and sanitation*', 6 October 2010, UNHRC Resolution 15/9, UN Doc. A/HRC/RES/15/9.

United Nations Human Rights Council, '*The human rights to safe drinking water and sanitation*', 5 October 2018, UNHRC Resolution 39/8, UN Doc. A/HRC/RES/39/8.

United Nations Mission in Kosovo, Regulation No. 2000/49 on the Establishment of the Administrative Department of Public Utilities, UNMIK/REG/2000/49 (19 August 2000).

United Nations News, *Water Access Critical to Beating Back COVID-19 Spread in Slum Areas* (23 March 2020).

United Nations Office for the Coordination of Humanitarian Affairs, '*Demolition and Seizure of Service Infrastructure in Palestinian Communities in Area C Exacerbates Risk of Forcible Transfer*', The Monthly Humanitarian Bulletin (September 2017).

United Nations Office of the High Commissioner for Human Rights, 'Information Received Concerning the Negative Impact on the Enjoyment of Human Rights and the Apparent Blockage of Aircraft and Vessels Carrying Essential Goods from Entering Yemen' (17 November 2016).

United Nations Security Council, *Letter dated 26 April 1991 from the Secretary-General addressed to the President of the Security Council*, UN Doc S/22535 (29 April 1991).

United Nations Security Council, *Report of the Second Panel Established Pursuant to the Note by the President of the Security Council of 30 January 1999 (S/1999/100), Concerning the Current Humanitarian Situation in Iraq*, UN Doc S/1999/356 (30 March 1999), Annex II.

United Nations Security Council, '*Kosovo*', 10 June 1999, UNSC Resolution 1244, UN Doc. S/RES/1244.

United Nations Security Council, '*Situation between Iraq and Kuwait*', 14 May 2002, UNSC Resolution 1409, UN Doc. S/RES/1409.

United Nations Security Council, '*Situation between Iraq and Kuwait*', 22 May 2003, UNSC Resolution 1483, UN Doc. S/RES/1483.

United Nations Security Council, '*Children and armed conflict*', 26 July 2005, UNSC Resolution 1612, UN Doc. S/RES/1612.

United Nations Security Council, '*Libya*', 16 September 2011, UNSC Resolution 2009, UN Doc. S/RES/2009.

United Nations Security Council, '*Middle East*', 21 October 2011, UNSC Resolution 2014, UN Doc. S/RES/2014.

United Nations Security Council, '*Central African Republic*', 28 January 2014, UNSC Resolution 2134, UN Doc. S/RES/2134.

United Nations Security Council, '*Middle East*', 14 July 2014, UNSC Resolution 2165, UN Doc. S/RES/2165.

United Nations Security Council, '*Threats to international peace and security caused by terrorist acts*', 13 February 2017, UNSC Resolution 2341, UN Doc. S/RES/2341.

United Nations Security Council, '*The situation in the Middle East*', 24 February 2018, UNSC Resolution 2401, UN Doc. S/RES/2401.

United Nations Security Council, '*Protection of civilians in armed conflict*', 24 May 2018, UNSC Resolution 2417, UN Doc. S/RES/2417.

United Nations Security Council, '*The situation in Libya*', 13 September 2018, UNSC Resolution 2434, UN Doc. S/RES/2434.

United Nations Security Council, '*The situation in Libya*', 12 September 2019, UNSC Resolution 2486, UN Doc. S/RES/2486.

United Nations Security Council, '*Threats to international peace and security*', 20 September 2019, UNSC Resolution 2490, UN Doc. S/RES/2490.

United Nations Secretary-General, 'Joint Statement by the Secretary-General and US Secretary of State John Kerry on Humanitarian Ceasefire Announcement' (31 July 2014).

United Nations Secretary-General, *Secretary-General's Appeal for Global Ceasefire* (23 March 2020).

United Nations Water, *Eliminating Discrimination and Inequalities in Access to Water and Sanitation*, Policy Brief (Geneva: UN Water, 2015).

United Nations Water and United Nations Educational, Scientific and Cultural Organization, *The United Nations World Water Development Report 2020: Water and Climate Change*, Report (Paris: UNESCO, 2020).

United States, Department of Defense, *Law of War Manual* (June 2015, updated December 2016).

United States, Joint Chiefs of Staff, *Joint Targeting*, Joint Publication 3–60 (31 January 2013).

United States Navy, *The Commander's Handbook on the Law of Naval Operations* (August 2017).

von Lossow, T., '*The Rebirth of Water as a Weapon: IS in Syria and Iraq*', 51:3, The International Spectator (2016) 82–99.

von Lossow, T., *Water as Weapon: IS on the Euphrates and Tigris*, SWP Comments 3 (Berlin: German Institute for International and Security Studies, 2016).

Western Front, Aerial Bombardment and Related Claims 1, 3, 5, 9–13, 14, 21, 25 and 26 (*Eritrea v. Ethiopia*), Partial Award, Separate Opinion of Hans Von Houtte (19 December 2005), 26 RIAA 291, 346–349.

World Health Organization, *Guidelines for Drinking Water Quality: Fourth edition incorporating the first addendum* (Geneva: WHO, 2017).

World Health Organization, *Health Conditions in the Occupied Palestinian Territory, including East Jerusalem, and in the Occupied Syrian Golan*, UN Doc A70/39 (22 May 2017).

World Health Organization, Regional Office for the Eastern Mediterranean, *Reconstruction of the Afghanistan Health Sector: A Preliminary Assessment of Needs and Opportunities* (Cairo: WHO, 2002).

World Meteorological Organization, 'World Meteorological Day focus on Climate Change and Water', Press Release (23 March 2020).

Zemmali, A., '*La protection de l'eau en période de conflit armé*', 77:815 International Review of the Red Cross (1995) 601–615.

www.ingramcontent.com/pod-product-compliance
Lightning Source LLC
Chambersburg PA
CBHW071354230926
51846CB00002B/544
9789004438286